D0032051

Biography: A Very Short Introduction

VERY SHORT INTRODUCTIONS are for anyone wanting a stimulating and accessible way into a new subject. They are written by experts, and have been translated into more than 45 different languages.

The series began in 1995, and now covers a wide variety of topics in every discipline. The VSI library now contains over 500 volumes—a Very Short Introduction to everything from Psychology and Philosophy of Science to American History and Relativity—and continues to grow in every subject area.

Titles in the series include the following:

Hermione Lee

BIOGRAPHY

A Very Short Introduction

OXFORD
UNIVERSITY PRESS

OXFORD
UNIVERSITY PRESS

Great Clarendon Street, Oxford OX2 6DP

Oxford University Press is a department of the University of Oxford.
It furthers the University's objective of excellence in research, scholarship,
and education by publishing worldwide in

Oxford New York

Auckland Cape Town Dar es Salaam Hong Kong Karachi
Kuala Lumpur Madrid Melbourne Mexico City Nairobi
New Delhi Shanghai Taipei Toronto

With offices in

Argentina Austria Brazil Chile Czech Republic France Greece
Guatemala Hungary Italy Japan Poland Portugal Singapore
South Korea Switzerland Thailand Turkey Ukraine Vietnam

Oxford is a registered trade mark of Oxford University Press
in the UK and in certain other countries

Published in the United States
by Oxford University Press Inc., New York

British Library Cataloguing in Publication Data
Data available

Library of Congress Cataloging in Publication Data
Data available

Typeset by SPI Publisher Services, Pondicherry, India
Printed in Great Britain by
Ashford Colour Press Ltd, Gosport, Hampshire

ISBN 978-0-19-953354-1

7 9 10 8

For Jenny Uglow

Biography

Who turned the page?
When I went out last night
his Life was left wide-open,
half way through, in lamplight on my desk:
The Middle Years.
Now look at him. Who turned the page?

Ian Hamilton

Contents

Acknowledgements

I am grateful to the following for various kinds of help, advice, inspiration, and information: John Barton; Dinah Birch; Elleke Boehmer; Michael Burden; Robert Faber; Roy Foster; Alex Harris; Hugh Haughton; Kathryn Holland; Ann Jefferson; Benjamin Lee; Amanda Lillie; Stephen Mulhall; Lucy Newlyn; Chris Pelling.

My deepest gratitude goes to my critical and affectionate readers, Julian Barnes and Jenny Uglow; my late, and much mourned, agent and friend, Pat Kavanagh; my editor at OUP, Andrea Keegan; the students with whom I have discussed biography and life-writing, at York and Oxford; and my husband John Barnard, for his unflagging encouragement of, and interest in, this book.

List of Illustrations

A Very Short Introduction

Biography has gone through many centuries of change, many variants and embodiments, and this book looks at a few of these in order to try and understand what biography does and how it works. Given the confines of a 'very short' book, it concentrates—though not exclusively—on British literary biography. Up to a point, it is structured chronologically. But it does not attempt to give a comprehensive survey of the genre, which would be a mind-numbing exercise.

Books or essays on biography often trace an evolutionary graph that goes from exemplary Lives or 'hagiographies', through to the vivid realism and intimacy of 18th-century portraits, to the conservative solidity of Victorian 'Lives and Letters', to modernist experiments with life-writing as an art form, and then rejoicingly on to the 'Golden Age' of long, professional, candid, post-Freudian 20th-century biography. Although these lines can, to an extent, be drawn, I find that kind of progressive model for biography misleading. What I see, rather, is the continual recurrence, in different contexts, of the same questions of definition, value, and purpose.

Chapter 1
The Biography Channel

Metaphors for biography

Biography is often compared to some other kind of thing, as
though it is difficult to fix it within a neat, single definition.
The terms used to describe what it is include Life, Life-history,
Life-writing, memoir, profile. Biography gets compared to
history (oral and written), to quests or journeys, detective work,
criminal trials, scenes in a play or the backstage of the theatre,
obituaries, encomiums, gossip, psychoanalysis, documentaries,
hauntings, burglary, embalmings, excavations, Oedipal conflicts,
betrayal, revenge, a broken bridge, a fishing-net, a work of fiction.

Of the many metaphors for biography, two make useful starting
points. One – a disturbing image – is the autopsy, the forensic
examination of the dead body which takes place when the cause
of death is unusual, suspicious, or ambiguous. The medical
examiner trained as a forensic pathologist opens up the corpse
(sometimes stripping the skin of the face right off the skull) and
employs his or her expertise in anatomy and pathology to
investigate, understand, describe, and explain what may have
seemed obscure, strange, or inexplicable. As one writer on
postmortems puts it, 'The property rights of the deceased to their
bodies terminate at the moment of death.' This process may not be
conclusive. Though the medical examiner is trained in scientific

methods and interpretation of the evidence, such expertise may not 'completely erase subjectivity...' 'The body does not lie – but the cause of death can still remain ambiguous.'

The metaphor of the autopsy invokes biography as a process of posthumous scrutiny, applied to a helpless subject from which life – or the soul, if you believe in a soul – has gone. The process cannot injure the person who is no longer there, but it can certainly change our posthumous view of them, depending on what is ascertained from the examination. And it can cause pain to surviving relatives and friends. The image of biography as a forensic process also suggests its limitations, since an autopsy can have nothing or little to say about the subject's thoughts, intelligence, emotions, temperament, talents, or beliefs. It may not even be able conclusively to prove the cause of death.

There is something gruesome about this metaphor. It is used when commentators on biography want to emphasize its ghoulish or predatory aspects. Henry James, shortly before his death, told his nephew (who was his executor) that his 'sole wish' was to 'frustrate as utterly as possible the postmortem exploiter' by burning a large number of his papers. Typically of those who think of biography as 'adding a new terror to death', he links the metaphor of the 'postmortem exploiter' to that of the grave-robber, adding that he had 'long thought of launching, by a provision in my will, a curse not less explicit than Shakespeare's own on any such as try to move my bones'.

A contrasting metaphor for biography is the portrait. Whereas autopsy suggests clinical investigation and, even, violation, portrait suggests empathy, bringing to life, capturing the character. The portraitist simulates warmth, energy, idiosyncrasy, and personality through attention to detail and skill in representation. Yet these two metaphors do have something in common. Portraits taken from life and posthumous autopsies both make an investigation of the subject which will shape how posterity views them. Both must pay precise attention to detail. Both can be revelatory. And the success of both depends on the practitioner's expertise and judiciousness.

When Hazlitt said in 1814 that 'portrait-painting is the biography of the pencil', he was using a commonplace analogy. The highest praise for a portrait (or a portrait-bust, or statue) is that 'the very life seems warm upon her lip', that it might be warm to the touch, 'looking as if she were alive'. So, 'catching a likeness' is a common phrase for what a biographer is trying to do. 'Warts and all' is another favourite phrase for what the ideally truthful biography should present. The subject of a biography, like that of a portrait, should seem to be alive, breathing, present in all the totality, there-ness, and authenticity of their being.

Biographers frequently use portraiture as an image for what they are doing. Plutarch compared his method of working to portrait-painters' concentration on the faces, and especially the expression in the eyes, of their subjects. Boswell said of Johnson, to their mutual friend the painter Joshua Reynolds, that Johnson 'has a peculiar art of drawing characters, which is as rare as good portrait-painting'. When he was writing his own *Life of Johnson*, Boswell drew on and made use of Reynolds' portraits of Johnson, and famously called his work 'the Flemish picture which I give of my friend...in which...I mark the most minute particulars.' The metaphor suggests biography's need to capture the 'vital spark' of the human subject, what Keats meant when he said 'The creature hath a purpose and its eyes are bright with it.' Thomas Carlyle, writing in the 1830s about the human sympathy that should fuel an ideal biography, spoke of catching the 'light-gleams' that make up a person's character.

The image of the portrait, though a more appealing one than the autopsy, also suggests what can go wrong with biography – flattery, idealization, flatness, inaccuracy, distortion. It makes us think, too, about the viewer's dependency on the artist's approach and technique. Another portrait might have given us a completely different idea of the subject. The possibilities for the representation of a self are infinitely various.

The metaphor has its limits. There are obvious differences between portraiture and biography: 'Biographical subjects . . . rarely stand still.' They speak, they change, they grow old, and they die.

1. **An image for biography: the portrait taken from life**

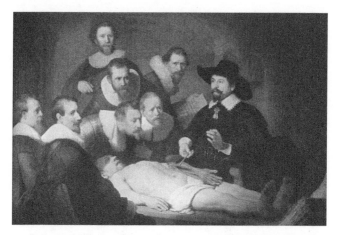

2. An image for biography: the forensic examination of a dead body

Definitions of biography

Is it possible to define biography without using metaphors or analogies? *The Oxford English Dictionary* of 1971 gives two definitions. The first, which now reads rather quaintly, is: 'The history of the lives of individual men, as a branch of literature' (the earliest example is from 1683, in Dryden's introduction to the *Lives* of Plutarch). The second is: 'A written record of the life of an individual' (first citation 1791). The *New Oxford Dictionary of English* of 2001 gives 'An account of someone's life written by someone else'. Here is another possibility: Biography is the story of a person told by someone else. Why 'story' rather than 'account'? Because biography is a form of narrative, not just a presentation of facts. Why 'told' rather than 'written'? After all, the word 'biography' literally means 'life-writing'. The two halves of the word derive from medieval Greek: *bios*, 'life', and *graphia*, 'writing'. But all biography involves an oral dimension – the recounting of memories, witness-testimony, much-repeated

5

anecdotes. And some forms of biography, such as documentary film, are not written.

Even this basic definition, 'the story of a person told by someone else', is unstable, and liable to exceptions. A biography could be written by the person whose story is being told, pretending to be someone else. Thomas Hardy, for instance, wrote his own biography, under the pretence it was being written by his wife. She finished it after his death, and it was published under her name. Gertrude Stein wrote her own biography as if it were being written by her partner, Alice B. Toklas, and called it *The Autobiography of Alice B. Toklas*. A biography of someone could be written by more than one person (the three-volume 1990s Cambridge University Press *Life of D. H. Lawrence* has a different author for each volume). A biography could be the story of several lives, not of one person. 'Group Lives', popular biographical enterprises in recent years (as in Jenny Uglow's *The Lunar Men*, or Megan Marshall's *The Peabody Sisters*) have a long history, though their predecessors usually took the form, not of several stories woven together in one narrative, but of short separate accounts of lives collected in a series or volume. A biography might tell the story of an animal or a thing rather than a person: there are biographies of cities, deities, and diseases, of Elizabeth Barrett Browning's spaniel Flush, of the Bayeux Tapestry, and of the River Thames.

Ten rules for biography

If definitions of biography need qualifying, what about rules? Here are ten possibilities.

1. The story should be true

Biographies of human beings are generally about real people, not fictional or mythological characters. Therefore the biographer has a responsibility to the truth, and should tell us what actually happened in the life. This looks like a solid, unarguable rule for biography. But there are many ways of breaking it. Plenty of biographers dramatize their narratives with descriptions of emotions, highly coloured scene-setting, or strategies of suspense. Some go further, and deploy full-scale fictional methods: invented meetings between author and subject, imaginary episodes, musings on the identity of the biographer, hypothetical conversations. Examples are A. J. A. Symons's *The Quest for Corvo: An Experiment in Biography* (1934), Ian Hamilton's *In Search of J. D. Salinger* (1988), Peter Ackroyd's *Dickens* (1990), and Edmund Morris's *Dutch: A Memoir of Ronald Reagan* (1999). Some biographies read more like fiction than history. This can attract readers, but can also give the genre a bad name. John Updike once remarked that most biographies are just 'novels with indexes'.

Even in the most sober and factual of biographical narratives, 'what actually happened' can be ambiguous or obscure. For some lives – such as the life of Jesus, or Shakespeare, or Cleopatra – there may be a vast mass of written or recorded utterances and a host of stories and legends, but little or no primary evidence. Where there is more first-hand or accredited evidence, there may often, also, be lies, exaggerations, and secrets. Biographers can spend a great deal of time sorting out the myths or false trails their subjects have created about their own lives. Witnesses, friends, and enemies have their own agendas, or misremember events, or embroider their anecdotes over the years. Biographers have to treat all testimony with scepticism and care. Untruths gather weight by being repeated and can congeal into the received version of a life, repeated in biography after biography until or unless unpicked. Some biographers settle on a single, possibly shaky hypothesis to explain a whole life: Richard Ellmann was criticized, for example, for maintaining on rather little evidence that Oscar Wilde had syphilis. Sometimes the truth about a person's life cannot be accessed: the evidence has been made away with, the witnesses are not there, the subject is mute. Then the true story would have to take the form of unanswerable questions or gaps in the record.

2. The story should cover the whole life

If a biography is to give you your money's worth ('A shilling life will give you all the facts', as Auden wrote), the expectation is that it will cover the whole story, or, in the case of a living subject, will go as far as it can. But attitudes have changed towards coverage. Until the 20th century, little detail was given about the childhood of the subject, unless to give anecdotes which pointed towards their behaviour in later life. The emphasis has shifted in the relative coverage of public achievements and domestic behaviour. Contemporary readers of biography expect to be given details about a subject's motives and fears, sexual habits, dealings with money, behaviour as a partner or parent, illnesses, peculiarities, even dreams or fantasies. Some, not all, biographers, spend time on their subjects' ancestors; some, not all, biographers track their subjects' posthumous lives and reputations.

If covering a 'whole life' implies that biography should proceed chronologically from cradle to grave, then this rule has been so often broken as not to count. Biographies can run backwards, can be organized by themes, can choose to dwell on certain key moments in a life, or can inter-cut their narratives with passages of history, literary criticism, description, or autobiography. Some biographies use a small part of a life-story to open out into the whole life. In *A Sultry Month: Scenes of London Literary Life in 1846* (1965), Alethea Hayter told the life-story of the Romantic painter Benjamin Haydon and of the group of writers and artists he knew by concentrating on the month in which Haydon died. *Wittgenstein's Poker* (2001) provided a dual mini-biography of Wittgenstein and Popper in 'the story of a ten-minute argument between two great philosophers'. James Shapiro chose the year 1599, 'a year in the life of William Shakespeare', as a way of capturing 'some of the unpredictable and contingent nature of daily life too often flattened out in historical and biographical works of greater sweep'. But this is not exclusively a modern method of writing biography. Lives of saints often spent far more

8

time on their martyrdoms than on their daily lives. Biographers who knew their subjects tended to concentrate on the parts of the life they had witnessed. Total coverage is not an invariable rule.

3. Nothing should be omitted or concealed

Contemporaneous readers of Western biography generally believe that there should be no censorship and no idealization, and that the value of the exercise of life-writing depends on its honesty and its thorough-going investigativeness. Even if it is hard to distinguish, at times, between a dislike of hypocrisy and a delight in scandal, the ethics of our society entail a belief in openness. This has partly to do with an increasing resistance to authority. We no longer want to treat leaders, monarchs, priests, or doctors with reverence, and we think their lives should be open to inspection. And the line we draw between the private and the public has changed. The ambivalent overlap between the 'public sphere' and the private life has been a contentious issue since the rise of mass media. In the late 20th and the 21st centuries, the presentation of the ordinary person's (as opposed to the famous person's) everyday private life for public consumption in Western culture has developed rapidly and dramatically out of new affordable technologies and media trends. Reality television, social networking websites, artwork dedicated to the banality of the private life, point to changing attitudes to what can be exhibited in public. These changes impinge on the writing of biography, always an index of its time. Mid to late 19th-century biography tended (with some exceptions) to censor sexual matters and what Johnson called 'domestick privacies'. We now regard such discretion, or hypocrisy, as unthinkable, unless a biography is being written of a recently dead subject with still-living relatives or close connections whose feelings have to be considered or who may threaten legal proceedings against the biographer if they feel they have been libelled. In such cases, exceptions to our codes of openness may be made.

Changing concepts of privacy and changing attitudes to censorship are not the only factors that affect biography's inclusiveness. Life is accumulation and repetition; narrative has to entail shaping and selection. Even a biography that appears to be omitting nothing – like Sartre's gigantic existential commentary on Flaubert's life, or Lockhart's voluminous, venerating life of Walter Scott, or Leon Edel's 'definitive' critical life of Henry James – has emerged from a process of choices.

4. All sources used should be identified

Biography is not a free zone. It is often involved with legal issues of property, permission, and copyright. A biography may be written at the request of an individual executor, or of a firm of publishers or agents acting for the subject's estate. Terms and conditions may be set up for the biographer which involve permission to use and quote certain materials. 'Unauthorized' biographers, who have not been asked to write about their subjects or who have not been granted such permissions, may find themselves unable to quote from, or having to paraphrase, key materials. Long before the concept of the authorized biography came into being, reputable biographers have preferred to authenticate their stories by referring to their sources or citing witnesses. So Plutarch would compare the different versions of a life-story he had derived from various authorities; Bede described the death of Saint Cuthbert by quoting at length from an eyewitness. From such early biographies right through to 20th-century biographies, witnesses are named and quoted, passages of testimony are infiltrated into the main narrative, the subject's own autobiographical writings are cited as evidence, and letters are used extensively, so much so that a genre called 'Life and Letters' emerged in the 19th century. (Biographers are often asked what effect the superseding of letters by email and texting will have on their work.) It was not until the 20th century, with the professionalization of biography and the emphasis on authenticity and verification, that extensive footnoting became the norm for biography, so that every reference could be checked. This professional convention, which is less than a hundred years old, seems to be on its way out. Trade publishers dislike footnotes: too academic, too space-consuming. Some historical biographers are solving this problem by putting their footnotes online, some popular biographers are minimizing their notes.

Citing one's sources is not always possible. An unauthorized biography of a still-living subject may make use of statements by witnesses who do not wish to be named. A biographer who has obtained materials from a source on condition of secrecy may not be able to disclose the name of the source. Authentication is desirable in biography, but it is not always the rule.

5. The biographer should know the subject

In early examples of biographical writing, centuries might elapse between the life of the subject and the writing of the Life. Plutarch was writing between about AD 98 and 125 about Greek leaders who lived in the 300s BC. Some medieval saints' Lives reached back over many centuries for the stories of their legendary subjects. Others – like a biography of Edward the Confessor commissioned by his widow – were written by near-contemporaries. Sir Thomas More wrote his critical history of Richard III, who died in 1485, in about 1513, only one generation on; More's son-in-law William Roper used his intimate knowledge of More in his memoir of him, written twenty years or so after his death. In the mid-17th century, Izaak Walton claimed a special virtue for his Lives of the Divines (including Donne and Herbert), written between 1640 and 1678, because he had either known them personally or had talked to those who did. A hundred years on, the belief that a biography could only be really valuable and useful if it were written by someone who had known the subject intimately was firmly held both by Dr Johnson and his biographer Boswell. 'Nobody can write the life of man', Johnson told Boswell, 'but those who have eat and drunk and lived in social intercourse with him.' Such personally connected biographical writing was much practised, and discussed, for good and ill, in the 19th century, when biography was often kept in the family. Not so now, when personal knowledge of or connection to the subject is not necessarily seen as an advantage or a requirement. The biographer who is asked to write the Life by the subject or by the subject's relations may find the authorization a heavy burden.

6. The biographer should be objective

The notion that biography can and should be impersonal and authoritative has always been in question. Early Lives of saints, martyrs, heroes, leaders, and thinkers frequently expressed opinions about their subjects, for good and ill. Life-writing from the 16th to the 18th centuries tended to be opinionated and partial, 19th-century biography often over-praised, 20th-century biography was often committed to a particular approach – notably the psychoanalytical method – which skewed the evidence. It has been argued – especially in the modernist period when an authoritative, public style for biography was being reacted against – that all biography is a form of autobiography. Even biographers who resist the notion that the story they are telling has anything to do with them, and put themselves in the narrative as little as possible, have to admit that their choice of subject has been made for a reason, and that there is no such thing as an entirely objective treatment. We write from a certain position, constructed by our history, nationality, race, gender, class, education, beliefs. More specifically, there is likely to be some shared experience between the writer and the subject. A drama critic might well write the life of an actor, a musicologist of a composer. It would be hard, if not impossible, to write a life of a mountaineer or a gardener, a chemist or an architect, with no experience – or at least no understanding at all – of those professions.

Biographers are often asked whether they like or love their subjects. If you are writing a biography of Hitler or Stalin or Attila the Hun, this is evidently not likely to be the case. Yet there will always be some emotion. The passion may be for the historical period or for the victims of the subject. The driving energy for the book may come from loathing or fear, a need to understand some monstrous career, or a revisionary desire to set the record straight.

Over-involvement, either way, can be counterproductive. Biographies written out of uncritical adulation can be as distorted as those that are motivated by punitive or revengeful motives. But biographies written without involvement, just as a money-making job or a duty, may fall flat. There must be some involvement, but there must also be detachment. Richard Holmes, the 'romantic' biographer of Coleridge and Shelley, put it memorably when he described biography as a broken bridge into the past:

> You stood at the end of the broken bridge and looked across carefully, objectively, into the unattainable past on the other side...For me, it was to become a kind of pursuit...You would never catch them; no, you would never quite catch them. But maybe, if you were lucky, you might write about the pursuit of that fleeting figure in such a way as to bring it alive in the present.

7. Biography is a form of history

'No man is an island, entire of it self; every man is a piece of the Continent, a part of the main.' 'No man lives without jostling and being jostled; in all ways he has to *elbow* himself through the world, giving and receiving offence... To paint a man's life is to present these things.' Donne is teaching his congregation about the individual's social responsibility, Carlyle is complaining about the over-delicate discretion of English biography, but both carry a message for biographers. There is no such thing as a life lived in isolation. In her 1920s, modernist spoof of 19th-century biographical conventions, *Orlando*, Virginia Woolf had fun with that biographical cliché 'the spirit of the age'. But, though she satirized the concept, she knew that one of biography's tasks is to place its subject in its 'age': the question is how best to do it. When she was thinking aloud about the difficulty of writing her memoir in her unfinished 'Sketch of the Past', in the late 1930s, she said of her own life: 'I see myself as a fish in a stream; deflected; held in place; but cannot describe the stream.' Biography, even more than autobiography (where the writer can choose how much to talk

13

about the world surrounding the self), has a duty to the stream as well as to the fish.

This is not only a matter of perspective or of narrative tactics. The relation of the individual to the age is also a political issue. Historians sometimes complain that biography is a misleading way of writing about the past. Concentration on an individual life distorts historical processes and can trivialize or over-personalize events. The political implications of prioritizing the life of an individual have been much debated. To set one Great Life centre-stage can be read as promoting a particular political agenda or as consolidating a hierarchical, anti-egalitarian social structure. The venerating and celebratory 19th-century lives of public figures have been called (by Michael Holroyd) 'part of the machinery for preserving the status quo'. The history of feminism, and of movements for racial equality, have a great deal to do with whose life-stories have been thought worth telling and how a life is told. Biography always reflects, and provides, a version of social politics, whether it is the nationalist agenda behind the collective biographical encyclopaedias of 19th-century France and England, or the post-Apartheid-era reactions which led to the biographical idealization of Nelson Mandela, or the changes in black cultural history in 20th-century North America which finally produced a full life of Ralph Ellison – whose *Invisible Man* was published in 1953 and who died in 1994 – in 2007. The popularity of certain kinds of biographies in different countries, periods, and cultures – biographies of saints or of naval heroes, of religious leaders, of footballers or rock-stars – provides an insight into that society. What does that society value, what does it care about, who are its visible – and invisible – men and women?

8. Biography is an investigation of identity

Since biography tells the story of a person, it requires, or assumes, a way of thinking about identity and selfhood. Writers of, and about, biography often discuss the best ways for biography to represent a self: shall it be through anecdote,

14

revelatory incidents, description, conversation, encounters with others, moments of decision-making, single acts, preferences, peculiarities, repeated habits? Any biographer must give some thought, even if not explicitly, to the relation of nature and nurture in the formation of a self, and to the negotiation between interior existence and the self's public performance.

It is not necessary for a biographer to have a theory or a set of general rules about identity – in fact, it can be a disadvantage. Biographers who succumb to the occupational temptation of using their subjects as a peg for generalizations about human behaviour can sound ponderous. Biographies that apply a specific theory of human behaviour – derived from Freud, or Bentham, or Marx, or Sartre – to the telling of a life-story, can retrospectively seem limited or simplifying. But in the writing of a life-story, some idea of how human beings function and what identity consists of is bound to emerge, though more often than not in an unsystematic or unexamined way.

Biography rubs up all the time against rival ways of understanding and explaining human beings and the nature of identity – psychoanalysis, philosophy, fiction, poetry, sociology, ethnography, history. Practitioners of those disciplines often have a hostile or sceptical attitude to biography: there are many examples of poems written against biography, especially in the 19th and 20th centuries, or of novelists treating biography with ironical suspicion or distaste (as in Henry James's *The Aspern Papers* or Julian Barnes's *Flaubert's Parrot*). Freud feared and distrusted biography (especially any that might be written of him) for its simplifications and over-conclusiveness. Proust argued against the critic Sainte-Beuve for belittlingly interpreting the works of his chosen writers through their life-stories. Yet Freud was fascinated – as in his case-study of Leonardo – by the possibilities of psychoanalytical biography, and Proust made his life's work a fiction which both resisted and invited biographical interpretation.

Biographers are not usually as explicit as philosophers such as Plato, Wittgenstein, Austin, or Moore on questions of the existence of an essential self, the extent to which a life can be lived according to a philosophical system, or the relation between acts and emotions. That is not their job – unless they are writing the Life of a philosopher. But biography is bound to reflect changing and conflicting concepts about what makes a self, what it consists of, how it expresses itself. The idea that there is such a thing as an innate, essential nature often vies in biographical narrative with the idea that the self is formed by accidents, contingencies, education, and environment. The idea that character can be designated as a type, or that human beings can be labelled by general, universal categories of identity, is more dominant in early biographies, and tends to give way, from the mid-18th century onwards, to an investment in individualism, originality, and specialness. The belief in a definable, consistent self, an identity that develops through the course of a life-story and that can be conclusively described, breaks down, to a great extent, in the late 19th and early 20th centuries, at a time when psychoanalysis, scientific discoveries such as the theory of relativity, and experiments in art forms, are producing a more indeterminate approach to identity. Western biography from this time has more to say about contradictions and fluctuations in identity, and about the unknowability of the self. But such contrasting ways of describing the self overlap and conflict, rather than following each other in a neatly chronological order.

9. The story should have some value for the reader

Biography raises moral issues. Its early, classical and Christian versions, presented their subjects as moral examples. A good life or a martyrdom provided a model for good behaviour or spiritual aspiration; a bad ruler or a fall from greatness provided an awful warning. This 'exemplary' strain in biography has never disappeared. A recurring argument is made for the usefulness of the genre. If biography can teach us how to live our lives, or can open our minds to lives very unlike our own, then it has an educational purpose: it is a branch of history and of knowledge. There are different and shifting opinions about how it can best fulfil this purpose. Biographers differ in their dedication to candour or 'veracity'; they ask whether small details or large acts are more eloquent ways of communicating character; they have varying views on whether the reader should be led to identify with recognizable, universal traits, or should be stirred or excited by examples of exceptional, unrepeatable behaviour. Is biography of more use if it provokes recognition and sympathy, or a sense of awe and unfamiliarity?

The opposite – and equally recurrent – approach to biography is to attack it for immorality. Words such as betrayal, violation, shame, prurience, intrusion, and exposure are applied to biography over a very wide historical time-span. Biography is attacked for breaching trust, violating privacy, trivializing a life's work, preying on its victim, simplifying a person's complexity, playing to our appetites for gossip and sensation. If biography is a form of scandal-mongering, then it is a low branch of the media and entertainment industry, and has no moral or educational value.

These opposing versions of the genre are not, in fact, mutually exclusive. Biography hovers between the two, sometimes within the same Life. Similarly, readers' motives may veer rapidly, almost simultaneously, between a high quest for inspiration and base, greedy curiosity. But whether biography is regarded as mainly moral or mainly immoral, what is not in doubt is its contemporary popularity. The telling of life-stories is the dominant narrative mode of our times. The popularity of Western biography has lasted for over two centuries, but in the last forty or fifty years – keeping pace with the relaxing of social conventions, increased social egalitarianism, the blurring of high and low art forms, and the cult of media celebrity – it has occupied new spaces. Biographies of politicians, sports and media stars; 'biopics' dramatizing the lives of Shakespeare or Elizabeth I, Kinsey or Truman Capote; television and film documentaries about a huge range of public figures; and the successful American cable television 'Biography Channel' are indications of how iconoclastic, socially wide-ranging, and non-literary biography has become. At the same time, biography has begun to be taken seriously by academics and literary theorists, and biography courses are offered in university departments of literature and history. Biography's current crossings-over between popular culture and literature, mass media and scholarship, may be due to social envy or social levelling, a media-fed gluttony for feeding off private lives, a longing for latter-day saints and heroes in an increasingly secularized society, a dumbing-down of readers who prefer the accessibility of a life-story to the hard work of poetry or literary fiction, or a desire to understand at least one individual's behaviour in a period of global confusion and uncertainty. Or to all or none of the above: perhaps, simply, to a persisting and universal appetite for stories.

10. There are no rules for biography

The instability of definitions and rules for biography suggest that it is a shape-shifting, contradictory, variable form. Yet, paradoxically, it can look like the most solid, conventional, and resistant to change of all forms of narrative. The adjective 'definitive' is often attached to biographies by hopeful publishers or enthusiastic reviewers. There is a lingering idea of biography as the complete, true story of a human being, the last word on a life. But if it is, rather, a mixed, unstable genre, whose rules keep coming undone, then perhaps the only rule that holds good is that there is no such thing as a definitive biography.

Chapter 2
Exemplary Lives

Here are some memorable episodes from the lives of six famous figures.

Moses, having led the people of Israel out of Egypt and given them the word from God over many years, is taken up to the top of Pisgah and shown the promised land. 'I have caused thee to see it with thine eyes' [the Lord says to him] 'but thou shalt not go over thither.' So he dies 'in the land of Moab' at the age of 'a hundred and twenty years', and there is 'weeping and mourning' for him for thirty days.

Socrates, who has been condemned to prison and death for introducing strange gods and corrupting the young, asks for the cup of hemlock to be brought. One of his disciples tells him there is plenty of time: many others have taken the poison late on their last day. 'Socrates said: It's reasonable for those you speak of to do those things – because they think they gain by doing them; for myself, it's reasonable not to do them; because I think I'll gain nothing by taking the draught a little later: I'll only earn my own ridicule by clinging to life ... Go on now; do as I ask, and nothing else.'

Alexander, Greek conqueror of the known world, goes to see the philosopher Diogenes, whose support he is seeking, and finds him 'relaxing in the sun'. He asks Diogenes if there is anything he wants. 'Yes,' replied Diogenes, 'move aside a little, out of my sunlight.' As Alexander is leaving with his retinue (who are all mocking the philosopher), he is heard to say: 'As for me, if I were not Alexander, I would be Diogenes.'

Just before he is captured, Jesus is praying in the garden of Gethsemane, asking his Father, 'if it be possible, to let this cup pass from me'. He has told his disciples to watch with him, but they fall asleep. 'And he cometh unto the disciples, and findeth them asleep, and saith unto Peter, What, could ye not watch with me one hour? Watch and pray, that ye enter not into temptation: the spirit indeed is willing, but the flesh is weak.'

The Roman Emperor Caligula, whose sadism, sexual appetites, extravagance, and perversity 'outdid that of all other prodigals ever', treats his horse Incitatus as a favourite. 'Apart from the marble stable, the ebony manger, the purple blankets and the gem-studded collar, he also gave him a house and a household of slaves and furniture ... It is said, too, that he meant to make him consul.'

Saint Jerome is sitting with his brother-priests in Bethlehem, hearing the holy lesson, when a lion suddenly comes limping into the monastery. All the other priests run away, but Saint Jerome receives the lion as if he were a guest. 'Than the lyon shewde his foot that was hurte to Seynt Jerom. Wherfore he callyd his brederyn ayen and badde hem waisshe the lyons foot and seke bysily where the sore was and so they dyd and they fonde that the sole of his foot was as hit had be woundyd and kut wyth knyves.' After they have cured him with their medicines, 'the lyon, levynge all his wyldnesse and fersnesse, dwellyd amonge theym as a tame best'.

These narratives cover many centuries. In some cases, there is a vast span of time between these versions of the story and the date of the story's origins; in others, only a few decades. Both the biblical stories are taken from the 1611 Authorized Version of the Bible. The earliest surviving versions of the Old Testament date from the 5th century BC; Matthew's gospel (which gives one of the several versions of the scene at Gethsemane) was written in the second half of the 1st century AD. Complete manuscripts of the New Testament have survived from the 4th century AD. Phaedo's account of the death of Socrates in 399 BC was written down by Plato between 371 and 367 BC. Alexander lived from 356 to 323 BC; his life-story is told by Plutarch between about AD 100 and 125. Caligula ruled Rome between AD 37 and 41; his horrifying regime is described by the Roman writer Suetonius in his *Lives of the Caesars*, written between AD 117 and 138. The cult of Saint Jerome began to take shape, long after his life in the 3rd to 4th centuries, in 9th-century Latin writings. This version is from Simon Winter's early 15th-century vernacular life.

The narratives these anecdotes are taken from could be classified as 'ur-biographies', primal forms of a genre that has not yet evolved. They all contain information about the births, dates, lives, and deaths of the subjects. But their structures are not what we would call biographical. They emphasize certain features – the teaching or the lessons provided by the subject, their legendary sayings, achievements, or crimes – and completely ignore others. They deal with time in a way that would be alien to more realistic life-stories, covering huge sweeps or marking only key events. They contain amazing 'facts' – such as Jesus's conversations with God, Moses' age at his death, or Jerome's friendship with his lion – which are presented without qualification or demurral. Of course, the Old Testament's poetic utterance of inscrutable events, Plutarch's sophisticated illustration of the weakness in pride and the split in one man between tyrant and philosopher, Suetonius's gleefully piled-up details about depravity, and the Jerome-historian's simple telling of the miraculous made ordinary, are very different from each other. But these narratives do have features in common. They describe human behaviour without providing motives or explanations. They want to impress the reader with the sense of a personality or an event of importance. All are interested in the effects of a life on others, whether disciples, victims, a nation, or posterity. They all use speech-acts to bring their messages home. There is no conception of a private or interior life: moments of solitude are witnessed by God; statements of belief or defining acts are performed in public. They all present their central figures, for good or ill, as exceptional and influential.

Western biography has its origins in such educational stories of remarkable men. (Or in stories from long before these examples, if you take the *Epic of Gilgamesh*, the tragic life and loves of the legendary Assyrian king who ruled in about 2600 BC, or the commemorative accounts of the Egyptian Pharaohs, as the first biographies.) The subjects of the classical writers are public figures, judged by their peers and posterity for their behaviour. Other classical life-writers whose work has endured are Xenophon, the 5th- to 4th-century BC Athenian who wrote a semi-fictional biography of the Persian king Cyrus and wrote vividly about Socrates; Theophrastus, Aristotle's pupil, who in about 319 BC wrote his *Characters*, short prose sketches of imaginary types like the Coward, the Drunkard, the Bore, and the Superstitious Man; and the Latin writer Cornelius Nepos, who, ahead of Plutarch, wrote some short *Lives of Illustrious Men* in the late 20s BC, also pairing Romans and Greeks. There are strong character-drawings by the Athenian historian Thucydides (c. 460–395 BC) and by the Roman historians Tacitus and Sallust. Greek and Roman literature contained many examples, also, of 'encomium', praise of the dead, and 'panegyric', praise for the living, two rhetorical forms of address which had a lasting effect on biography.

The main events of classical lives are battles, conquests, victories in government and argument, dominance over the populace, the imparting of wisdom, influential deeds and sayings. (Though Plutarch, a richly varied writer, is also interested in personal detail and domestic anecdotes.) Sometimes, as in Plutarch, they are paralleled, so that one character stands out in relief against another: so the mercurial Greek charmer Alcibiades is paired with the stubborn, proud Roman Coriolanus. Sometimes, as in

Suetonius, good and bad characteristics are piled up in turn. But there is a standard pattern, beginning with early signs of character revealed in childhood incidents, followed by a rising trajectory, illustrated by exploits, sayings, or revealing examples of behaviour. The Lives reach a plateau of status, influence, success, wealth, or power, and then fall or decline, through errors of judgement, unpopularity, conspiracy, defeat, exile, betrayal, disgrace, or senility. The death scenes – like Plato's of Socrates or Suetonius's of Nero – can have a powerful impact. These lives are written with a moral purpose, but also to entertain. They have a political agenda – Plutarch's, for instance, to consolidate links between the Greeks and the Romans.

Plutarch, much influenced by Aristotle, is a writer with a moral purpose. In his *Life of Pericles* he says that 'actions arising out of virtue . . . immediately put one in a frame of mind such that one simultaneously admires the acts and desires to emulate the agents'. He constantly drew exemplary, generalized lessons from individual lives. He showed that character could be shaped and changed through accidents, catastrophes, and successes. But he also believed there was such a thing as innate character. His treatment of that brilliant slippery character Alcibiades is a case in point:

> Of the many skills Alcibiades possessed, we hear in particular of one which was a useful tool for captivating men, and that was that he could assimilate and adapt himself to their habits and lifestyles . . . In Sparta he took exercise, lived frugally, and wore a frown on his face; in Ionia he was fastidious, companionable, and easy-living; in Thrace he went in for hard drinking and hard riding . . . It was not that he actually changed personality so readily, or that his character was infinitely mutable, but . . . he assumed and took refuge in whatever appearance and image was appropriate for [the people he was with].

Not all Plutarch's subjects lead to a single moral: many are complicated, inconsistent, and profoundly flawed.

Plutarch was writing about long-past lives, which he wanted to bring vividly to life, but he famously distinguished what he was doing from the work of a historian.

> I am not writing history but biography, and the most outstanding exploits do not always have the property of revealing the goodness or badness of the agent; often, in fact, a casual action, the odd phrase, or a jest reveals character better than battles involving the loss of thousands upon thousands of lives ... Just as a painter reproduces his subject's likeness by concentrating on the face and the expression of the eyes ... I must be allowed to devote more time to those aspects which indicate a person's mind. ... while leaving their major exploits and battles to others.

This kind of life-writing had a lasting influence. Between the 15th and the 17th centuries, Plutarch was translated into Latin, then French, then English. Shakespeare based his Roman plays on Thomas North's 1579 translation. His popularity in Britain continued all through the 18th and 19th centuries. Dryden explained Plutarch's appeal in 1683, in the preface to a new translation, not primarily as a moralist, but as a creator of character who takes you behind the scenes:

> Here you are led into the private lodgings of the hero: you see him in his undress, and are made familiar with his most private actions and conversation. You may behold ... Augustus playing at bounding-stones with boys; and Agesilaus riding on a hobby-horse among his children. The pageantry of life is taken away; you see the poor reasonable animal, as naked as nature ever made him; are made acquainted with his passions and his follies, and find the Demi-God a man.

Plutarch's achievement, according to Dryden, is to have humanized his great men. That is not the main aim of the other major strand of 'ur-biographies', the saints' Lives, or hagiographies. (The term derives from Late Latin *hagiographa*, from Greek '*agios*', holy, and '*graphia*', writing.) These are lives lived in imitation of Christ, in retreat from the world, dedicated to God, providing lessons in exceptional godliness and purity. In the standard pattern, they start with early signs of spirituality shown through childhood incidents, followed by a break, often violent and difficult, with worldly connections (family, society, politics, government), perhaps a conversion, and a commitment to a holy life. The narrative then settles down to giving examples of the holy person's sayings, conversations, visions, and miracles, culminating in a farewell address, a holy death or martyrdom, miraculous posthumous proofs of sainthood, and evidence of lasting influence. The saints' trials – testing of virginity, conflicts with pagan authorities, torture, imprisonment – are always emphasized, and a good death is a key part of the story. As classical Lives emphasized traits and provided 'exempla' of types of behaviour, saints' Lives displayed prototypical virtues.

Hagiography was 'one of the dominant literary genres in Europe from Late Antiquity to the end of the Middle Ages'. It covers an enormous time-span, from Latin and Greek texts written by, and for, monks, to vernacular versions, probably for a lay audience, between the 13th and the 15th centuries. Saints' Lives run from early examples such as the anonymous Life of Cuthbert, written in about 699 by a monk of Lindisfarne (improved on by Bede when he came to write his Life of Cuthbert in the 720s) and Aelfric's Old English *Lives of the Saints*, written around AD 1000; to 11th- and 12th-century Anglo-Norman saints' Lives in verse; and 13th- and 14th-century collections such as the *South England Legendary* or Jacobus de Voragine's *Legenda Aurea, The Golden Legend*. They generally become more psychologically complex over time, more interested in the saints' conversions and self-doubts than in lists of miracles. After the 15th century, the dominance of hagiography fades away, but it persists in 19th-century collections of Protestant martyrs, such as *English Female Worthies*; 20th-century compilations of *Saints and Sinners*; modern lives of Catholic heroes such as Evelyn Waugh's Life of

Edmund Campion; and sanctified accounts of contemporary public figures like Martin Luther King or Mother Theresa. The most famous saints' Lives were repeatedly rewritten, collecting additional anecdotes along the way. Saint Catherine, the daughter of a king who challenged and defeated the Emperor Maxentius and his philosophers in arguments over sacrificing to pagan gods, who refused to marry Maxentius or to be worshipped as a statue, who was to be tortured on a knife-studded wheel except that angels broke it in bits, and who when eventually beheaded spouted milk, not blood, was supposedly martyred in 4th-century Alexandria. But her cult as the 'pre-eminent virgin martyr', bride of Christ, and patron of nuns, philosophers, wheelwrights, and wet-nurses, only developed from the 10th century, when the earliest known Greek and Latin versions of her story were written, coinciding with the discovery of relics and the building of shrines. As she became increasingly popular, later versions embroidered her qualities. Those written for clerics spent more time on her philosophical arguments; lay versions concentrated on her routing of the opposition and her miracles. In some retellings, she was courtly, witty, and brilliant; in others, she was rude and fierce – as here, refusing to be made into an object of worship: 'Be stylle, thou fool! I saye to thee,/Thou redes me to ful mekyl synne!/What man wolde idampnyd be/In helle for ony worldys wynne?/I have to Jhesu Cryst my love:/He is my spouse, bothe oute and inne.'

Saints' Lives served many purposes. They boosted cults, shrines, and the sale of relics. They encouraged piety and spirituality. They created links, in their vernacular versions, between ordinary people and the church. They had complex political and social agendas, including critiques of contemporary life, lessons in manners, sexual roles, and economics, and even religious dissent. Their subjects were 'rebels, failed monarchs, disobedient children, virginal spouses, social radicals and cross-dressers'. Like Catherine, they could be caustic, defiant, and bossy. There were many 14th-century examples in which 'witty, resilient saints make fools of the bumbling authorities who try to intimidate or to harm

3. A famous saint's dramatic martyrdom

them'. These lives were 'often more exemplary than imitable'. They are the starting point for the tension that biography produces between wanting to identify and emulate, and wanting to know about a life inconceivably different to one's own.

In Reformation England, hagiography became contested territory. Protestantism created its own saints (as in John Foxe's gigantic *Actes and Monuments*, better known as the *Book of Martyrs*, begun in 1563, or Milton's Sonnet of 1655 on the 'slaughtered saints',

Protestants massacred in Piedmont). The humanism and scepticism of the Renaissance or Early Modern period, its explorations and experiments in the arts and sciences, its passion for classical learning, and its interest in individualism, belief systems, and political structures involved fresh ways of thinking about life-writing. Hagiography came under attack as a form of superstitious ideology. By the 17th century, Thomas Fuller, in his Protestant biographical compendium of English types, *Worthies of England* (1662), was pouring scorn on the 'forgeries' and 'grand abuse' to be found in the Lives of Saints, due to the 'want of honest hearts in the *Biographists* of these saints' – and the profit they earned for pilgrimage sites. His prejudices come through strongly in his account of King Alfred, who 'loved religion more than superstition; favoured learned men more than lazy monks; which, perchance, was the cause that his memory is not loaded with miracles, and he not solemnly sainted with other Saxon kings who far less deserved it'.

Hagiography became a bad word. Especially for historians of biography at the start of the 20th century, reacting against what they saw as the Victorians' resurrection of saintly Lives, pre-Reformation life-writing looked like a black hole. Edmund Gosse's entry on 'Biography' in the 11th edition of the *Encylopaedia Britannica* (1910–11) pronounced: 'Biography hardly begins to exist in English literature until the close of the reign of Henry VIII'. Later commentators followed suit. Recent surveys refer to 'the darkness of hagiography' holding biography in thrall over 'a thousand years of saints' lives', of the 'dark ages' of 'a church-policed culture of veneration'. Modern readers do not expect biography to be programmed and polemical. We prefer, retrospectively, the classical strain of life-writing as described by Dryden, the revelation of the 'poor reasonable animal' in undress, and are frustrated by hagiography's 'conventional formulas, polemical exaggerations, and shameless borrowings'.

Exemplary Lives came to be seen as narratives of representative types, and it is often said that biography develops into the genre we know with the emergence of an interest in individualism in the 16th and 17th centuries. The range of subjects thought appropriate for a Life broadened with the rise of the middle classes and with social movements towards democracy. By the later 17th and 18th centuries, more 'private' Lives were being written and much more emphasis was being placed on ideas of selfhood and the autonomy of the individual.

But these tidy progressive histories of biography are not fool-proof. Neither classical Great Men's lives nor medieval saints' Lives presented uncomplicated models of exemplarity. They are also interested in providing moral instruction through dramatic examples of bad behaviour and unsuitable models for ordinary life, accompanied by awful warnings. Secular collections like Lydgate's *Fall of Princes*, derived from Boccaccio in the 1430s, told ominous stories of great men tumbling down as the Wheel of Fortune turns. *The Mirour for Magistrates*, a collection of verse-lives (in editions from 1555 to 1587), provided 'tragicall examples' of how 'this weltring world, both flowes and ebs like seas'. Destinies were summed up ('How Thomas Wolsey did arise unto great authority and government, his maner of life, pompe, and dignity, and how hee fell down into great disgrace, and was arested of high treason'), characters lamented their own fates as if from beyond the grave, and bitter lessons were drawn: 'How frayle al honours are, how brittle worldly blisse.'

As in *The Mirour for Magistrates*, the two strands of worldly classical Lives and Christian hagiography did not form clear-cut, separate influences on modern biography. The complicated intertwining of pagan and Judaeo-Christian stories is seen, for example, in the strange biographical mutations of Alexander, via Greek, Latin, Hebrew, Arabic, Spanish, and French sources in late antiquity and the early Middle Ages, from Greek conqueror of the East to chivalric Christian hero of medieval romances. A mixed lineage of classical leaders' speeches and Christian saints' oratory combined to influence the 'rhetorical performances' of 17th-century life-writings. The pre-history of biography leaves a complicated and long-lasting legacy. It is misleadingly neat to argue that classical models were overturned by the dark ages of hagiography, thankfully superseded by secular, democratic candour and idiosyncrasy. Exemplary representations of lives with universally recognizable traits did not suddenly disappear; they persisted into the 18th and 19th centuries. The idea of an exemplary life has never gone away.

Francis Bacon, politician and philosopher under Elizabeth and James I, famously divided History into three branches: Chronicles of the age, Lives, and Narrations of specific actions. He preferred Lives. Because they told of a single person 'in whom actions both greater and smaller, public and private, have a commixture', they ought, if well written, to contain 'a more true, native, and lively representation'. But he found it strange, in 1605, 'that the writings of lives should be no more frequent ... yet are there many worthy personages ... that deserve better than dispersed report or barren eulogy'.

There were a few exceptions which could have proved him wrong, but some of them were only circulating in manuscript: it was dangerous to publish accounts of recently dead monarchs and leaders. Sir Walter Raleigh, writing his *History of the World* from the Tower, knew that 'whosoever in writing a modern Historie shall follow truth too neare the heeles, it may haply strike out his teeth'. George Cavendish's lavishly descriptive tragic life of his employer Cardinal Wolsey (who died in 1561) was circulating long before it was printed in 1641. Sir Thomas More's *History of Richard III*, written in the 1510s but not published in full until 1557, made a vigorous, ironic, highly dramatized critique of the wicked monarch and in passing gave a sympathetic character-sketch of Jane Shore, Edward IV's 'concubine', with a note defending the value of setting so 'slight a thing' 'among remembrances of great matters'. Its story broke off before getting too close to the present. William Roper's memoir of his father-in-law Thomas More was written in the 1550s, about twenty years after More's death in 1535, and was privately circulated before being printed in 1626. Because he had lived in his household for many years, Roper could give an inward, authentic picture of More's character, with all his turns of speech. So we hear More trying to explain to his wife Alice why she should not mind his imprisonment. Clearly not his intellectual equal, she meets his philosophy with her usual kind of 'homely' brush-off: ' "Is not this house," quoth he, "as nighe heaven as my owne?" To whom shee, after hir accustomed homely fashion ... awneswered, "Tylle valle, Tylle valle!" '. And we see him going wisely and humorously to his death: 'I pray you, master Leiuetenaunte, see me salf [safe] uppe, and for my cominge downe let me shifte for my self.'

By the end of the 17th century, those sorts of vivid individualistic lives, almost a match for Thomas More's portraitist Holbein in depth, intensity, and telling detail, were no longer the exception in English and European life-writing. Montaigne's autobiographical writings of the 1580s and 1590s about the self and its complexities (first translated into English in 1603), preceded a flurry of vividly individualized 17th-century French memoirs, letters, and literary anecdotes, running alongside the formal, classical tradition of the *éloge*, which were increasingly being written in French rather than in Latin – a collection of *Éloges des hommes savants*, for instance. In Italy, Benvenuto Cellini's autobiography, though not published until 1730, was being written, between 1558 and 1566, at a time when vernacular collections of biographies – like the Florentine Vespasiano da Bisticci's lives of leaders and writers, or Giorgio Vasari's *Lives of the Most Excellent Italian Architects, Painters and Sculptors* (1550, 1568) – were displacing the earlier, classically influenced collections of short 'illustrious' lives in Latin by 14th-century writers such as Petrarch and Villani. Vasari's *Lives* established a

4. Depth, intensity, detail: a great 17th-century-biographical portrait

powerful convention of talking about works of art biographically, through the personality of the artist.

Biographical writing in 17th-century England was energized, just as much as Petrarch or Montaigne or Vasari, by classical models, through Thomas North's translation of Plutarch's *Lives* in 1579 and new translations of Theophrastus, Tacitus, and Suetonius. But it

THE LIVES

OF THE NOBLE GRE-

CIANS AND ROMANES, COMPARED

together by that graue learned Philosopher and Historiogra-
pher, Plutarke of Chæronea:

Translated out of Greeke into French by IAMES AMYOT, Abbot of Bellozane,
Bishop of Auxerre, one of the Kings priuy counsel, and great Amner
of Fraunce, and out of French into Englishe, by
Thomas North.

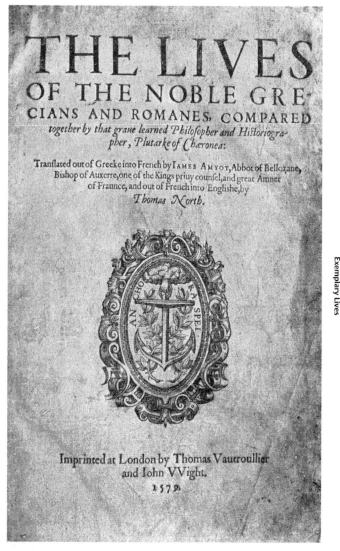

Imprinted at London by Thomas Vautroullier
and Iohn VVight.
1579.

5. Classical lives: the rise and fall of great men

reached beyond its origins. It covered a wide, contemporaneous range of subjects – rulers, magistrates, worthies, artists, poets, churchmen, thinkers – and took many forms. There were individual Lives, collective group Lives, biographical dictionaries, obituaries, 'memoirs, diaries, epistolary collections, hagiographies, character-sketches and royal lives'. Praise and eulogy were mixed with criticism and satire, universal types with curious individuals, formal rhetorical patterns with eccentric deviations. Empirical scientific discoveries and explorations of the natural world, notably by members of the Royal Society such as Robert Hooke and Robert Boyle, impinged on ideas of how a human life might be investigated. Locke's enquiries towards the end of the century into the workings of the mind changed the next generation's thinking about the formation of identity. Hierarchies of high and low, public and private, were shifting. The traditions of saints' Lives and classical Lives began to mingle in life-writing with quite different genres: scandal-sheets, crime reports, satirical poetry, family portraits.

As the writing of Lives became more diverse, the word 'biography' came into general use – first with Fuller's use of 'biographist' in 1662, then with Dryden's category, in his 1683 introduction to Plutarch, of 'biographia, or the history of particular men's lives'. Biography began to be discussed as a genre. Two famous examples of collective Lives show how differently it could be done. Izaac Walton's serious celebrations of the poet-priests Donne and Herbert, the politician Henry Wotton, and the theologians Richard Hooker and Robert Sanderson, written and much re-written between 1640 and 1678, fused together a number of the available ways of thinking about 'good men': hagiographies and martyrologies, panegyrics and encomiums, funeral sermons, commemorations, and portraiture, Theophrastian character-sketches, and books on 'ars moriendi', the art of dying, giving advice on 'Dyenge Well' or 'Good Deaths'. Walton was carefully read by both Johnson and Boswell. Later, he came to be over-idealized as a saintly writer, and then dismissed for inaccuracy. One 19th-century biographer of Herbert attacked Walton's Lives

Corporis hæc Animæ fit Syndon Syndon Jesu
Amen

's R. scup And are to be sould by R R and Ben: ffisher

6. Donne: the death-bed portrait

as a 'mingle-mangle of unhistoric statement and mendacious zeal'. But his loving respect and, in some cases, personal feeling for his subjects, and his copious use of their own words, gave his exemplary Lives an intimate sense of personality. He did not make high claims for his own work; he was making 'the best plain Picture' that he could, and he thought what he was doing was 'usefull'.

Walton ends his *Life of Donne* with visual comparisons. On his death-bed, Donne asked to be wrapped in his winding-sheet, to have a portrait made of his 'lean, pale and death-like face', which he kept by him till the hour of his death. Walton compares this image to Donne's portrait as a young man and to his commemorative marble statue in St Paul's, so like Donne that 'it seems to breath faintly'. He ends with his own 'picture' of Donne, drawn according to the science of physiognomy: 'His aspect was cheerful, and such as gave a silent testimony of a clear knowing soul . . . His melting eye showed that he had a soft heart, full of noble compassion.' Walton concludes with a pious hope which also sums up what he has been trying to do. The body which he has been describing 'is now become a small quantity of Christian dust'. 'But I shall see it reanimated.'

Those eloquently written, carefully structured, reverential memoirs could not be more different from *Brief Lives*, the amoral, forthright, energetic, and scrappy life-writings of John Aubrey, dating from the 1670s and 1680s. Typically of an inquiring man of his time – like Pepys, whose diaries were contemporaneous – Aubrey was interested in everything: antiquarianism, archaeology, astrology, horticulture, mathematics, folklore, dreams, ghosts, horoscopes, heraldry. Biography, for him, was just another branch of natural science. But Aubrey was, also, wildly disorganized. He called his four hundred or so biographical sketches, a mixture of anecdotes, gossip, memories, and observations, 'skediasmata', 'scattered things' (or, in the phrase of his later biographer, the novelist Anthony Powell, 'pieces written on the spur of the moment'). They were written in no particular order, often in bits or unfinished, as a collaboration with the antiquarian Anthony à Wood (the most vain and vindictive of Oxford scholars) for his *Athenae Oxonienses*, an encyclopaedia of all the writers and bishops educated at Oxford from 1500 to 1690. Aubrey told Wood in 1680 that he thought life-writing should be candid and truthful, but that there were risks attached.

> I here lay-downe to you ... the Trueth ... the naked and plaine trueth, which is here exposed so bare that the very pudenda are not covered, and affords many passages that would raise a Blush in a young Virgin's cheeks. So that after your perusall, I must desire you to make a Castration ... and to sowe-on some Figge-leaves ... These Arcana are not fitt to lett flie abroad, till about 30 yeares hence, for the author and the Persons (like Medlars) ought to be rotten first.

Wood betrayed his trust and got Aubrey into hot water. They quarrelled bitterly, and Aubrey's work was published only piecemeal or in expurgated form until the 20th century. Even so, his commitment to the naked truth played an important part in biography's long debate between 'veracity' and discretion; his lively, gossipy miniaturism had an influence on later 'short lives' like Marcel Schwob's *Vies Imaginaires* or Lytton Strachey's *Eminent Victorians*, and his magpie eye for revealing details of behaviour and speech anticipated the 18th century's passion for anecdotes and 'ana'.

Aubrey liked to mix up his life-stories with theories about human behaviour, superstitions, general opinions, and accounts of how he came by his information. One Brief Life ends: 'He dyed of a broaken heart.' Telling of a youthful drunken exploit by the poet John Denham, who once blotted out with ink all the road-signs between Temple Bar and Charing Cross, he noted that he 'had [the story] from R. Estcott, Esq., that carried the Inke-pott'. A life of a famous beauty, Venetia Digby, whose memorial bust he later spotted standing outside a shop in Newgate Street, with the gilding peeled off, provoked the comment: 'How these curiosities would be quite forgott, did not such idle fellowes as I am putt them downe.' He had a brilliant gift for rapidly invoking character. Francis Bacon, baldly described (in Greek lettering) as a paederast, had 'a delicate, lively, hazel Eie; Dr Harvey told me it was like the Eie of a viper'. Hobbes, who gets the longest Life, had a habit of singing aloud at night, when 'he was sure nobody heard him' from his book of prick-songs (vocal music): 'He did beleeve it did his Lunges good, and conduced much to prolong his life'. Aubrey could get carried away with a particularly juicy story (of the kind that had to be fig-leafed by his 19th-century editor):

Biography

[Sir Walter Raleigh] loved a wench well; and one time getting up one of the Mayds of Honour up against a tree in a Wood...who seemed at first boarding to be something fearfull of her Honour, and modest, she cryed, sweet Sir Walter, what doe you me ask? Will you undoe me? Nay, sweet Sir Walter! Sweet Sir Walter! Sir Walter! At last, as the danger and the pleasure at the same time grew higher, she cryed in the extasey, Swisser Swasser Swisser Swasser. She proved with child, and I doubt not but this Hero tooke care of them both, as also that the Product was more than an ordinary mortal.

And he could not resist a good joke:

Edward de Vere. Born 1550. He was a courtier of Queen Elizabeth, who lost his friends by his insolence and pride, and his fortune by his extravagance...This Earle of Oxford, making of his low obeisance to Queen Elizabeth, happened to let a Fart, at which he was so abashed and ashamed that he went to Travell, 7 yeares. On his returne the Queen welcomed him home, and sayd, My Lord, I had forgott the Fart.

We have come a long way from the fate of Moses to the fart of Edward de Vere: but biography continues to mix together those contradictory strains, the epic and the absurd, legends and gossip, the elegiac and the anecdotal, gravity and foolishness.

Chapter 3
Warts and All

Samuel Johnson (aged 64) and James Boswell (aged 33) are travelling together in the Hebrides, in the autumn of 1773. It is ten years since they first met in London. They are staying, in company, on the Isle of Skye.

> We danced tonight to the musick of the bagpipe, which made us beat the ground with prodigious force. I thought it better to endeavour to conciliate the kindness of the people of Sky, by joining heartily in their amusements, than to play the abstract scholar. I looked on this Tour to the Hebrides as a copartnership between Dr. Johnson and me. Each was to do all he could to promote its success; and I have some reason to flatter myself, that my gayer exertions were of service to us. Dr. Johnson's immense fund of knowledge and wit was a wonderful source of admiration and delight to them; but they had it only at times; and they required to have the intervals agreeably filled up, and even little elucidations of his learned text. I was also fortunate enough frequently to draw him forth to talk, when he would otherwise have been silent. The fountain was at times locked up, till I opened the spring.

This is from Boswell's *Journal of a Tour to the Hebrides*, published in 1785, a year after Johnson's death, and twelve years after their journey. Johnson had published his own version of the tour, *A Journey to the Western Islands of Scotland*, in 1775. The two versions are – as Boswell's biography would be – a form of

7. **Reynolds' Johnson: The man of letters, warts and all**

THE

L I F E

OF

SAMUEL JOHNSON, LL.D.

COMPREHENDING

AN ACCOUNT OF HIS STUDIES AND NUMEROUS WORKS,

IN CHRONOLOGICAL ORDER;

A SERIES OF HIS EPISTOLARY CORRESPONDENCE
AND CONVERSATIONS WITH MANY EMINENT PERSONS;

AND

VARIOUS ORIGINAL PIECES OF HIS COMPOSITION,

NEVER BEFORE PUBLISHED.

THE WHOLE EXHIBITING A VIEW OF LITERATURE AND LITERARY MEN
IN GREAT-BRITAIN, FOR NEAR HALF A CENTURY,
DURING WHICH HE FLOURISHED.

IN TWO VOLUMES.

By JAMES BOSWELL, Esq.

——— *Quò fit ut* OMNIS
Votiva pateat veluti defcripta tabella
VITA SENIS.———   HORAT.

VOLUME THE FIRST.

LONDON:
PRINTED BY HENRY BALDWIN,
FOR CHARLES DILLY, IN THE POULTRY.
M DCC XCI.

8. Boswell's Johnson: still the most famous of all British biographies

'copartnership', often giving different accounts of the same events. Boswell's *Journal* was also a trailer for his long-awaited *Life* of Johnson. He noted in the *Journal* that in 1773 he was asking Johnson 'particulars of his life, from his early years', and was planning to 'collect authentick materials for *The Life of Samuel Johnson, LLD*'. He had 'a vast treasure of his conversation', and planned to make up for not having known him earlier by 'assiduous enquiry'. The *Life* finally appeared in 1791, twenty-eight years after their first meeting and seven years after Johnson's death.

Boswell dancing and Johnson talking on the Isle of Skye introduce the dynamics, and the comedy, of their biographical relationship. Those who (at the time and later) found Boswell chattering, prancing, and self-promoting, and Johnson uncouth, severe, and overbearing, always made fun of the 'copartnership'. Boswell has been much blamed for dancing in front of his subject. The *Tour*, said Horace Walpole, making Johnson and Boswell into Don Quixote and Sancho Panzo, was the story of 'a mountebank and his zany'. The *Life*, said the hostile Thomas Macaulay, forty years after its publication, was a great book inexplicably written by a feeble-minded laughing-stock about 'a mind at least as remarkable for narrowness as for strength'. Boswell's absurdity and Johnson's grotesqueness have always been mixed up with the epic, even tragic, dimensions of what is still the most famous (even if, now, not the most widely read) biography in the English language.

It is such a strange book to stand as the classic example of the genre. Why should an eccentric, passionately opinionated, bullying, neurotic 18th-century lexicographer, biographer, and journalist be the most famous hero of British life-writing? And why should an enormous, garrulous hold-all of a narrative be the pre-eminent model of biography? Though the *Life* is chronological, it spends far more time on the period during which Boswell knew Johnson than on the preceding fifty-four years of Johnson's life: half the book covers Johnson's last eight years. Because Boswell was a slow and disorganized worker, several other accounts of

Johnson were published before his, so he is constantly slapping down his rivals and promoting his own account as the most 'authentick'. Because his 'assiduous enquiry' produced a mountain of testimonies and documentation, he puts chunks of Johnson's letters and other people's letters and anecdotes in between his own stories of Johnson's behaviour, descriptions of social occasions, and transcriptions (or imitations) of Johnson's conversation and sayings. His own relationship with Johnson is much the most prominent of Johnson's friendships. Though he promises 'veracity' – about himself as well as his subject – he also omits some details, for instance about Johnson's peculiar marriage or his feelings for women.

Since the discovery of an amazing cache of Boswell's papers in the 1920s, and the growth of a huge scholarly industry on Boswell and Johnson, much work has been done to show how carefully and artfully shaped the *Life* really is. Meanwhile, Johnson has been rescued from Boswell, in biographical works that go back to the young, pre-Boswellized Samuel Johnson, or look at him through other eyes – for instance, those of his women writer friends such as Hester Thrale and Fanny Burney – or in editions of his works, notably of his own major biographical enterprise, the *Lives of the English Poets*. Yet Boswell continues to dance at the centre of the British biographical stage.

Boswell's Life of a man of letters emerged from a century in which there was a massive expansion of print and reading in Britain. The democratization and secularization of knowledge, the growing dominance of realistic fiction as a popular genre, the increasing variety of available reading materials, involved a book trade and a literary market place (mainly centred on London) of the utmost energy, competitiveness, brutality, and complexity. Boswell and Johnson were both deeply embedded in this Grub Street world of professional, money-making hack-work, and part of the interest of Boswell's *Life* is that it gives such a detailed account of, yet seems to rise above, its context. Literary patronage, literary rivalry, and literary reputations were the driving forces, and also, often, the subject matter, for many writers. A highly socialized, gossipy, backbiting, and rivalrous literary world structured itself through clubs, magazines, reviews, and literary groups. Writers met in public, sat in coffee houses, talked in salons, walked the streets and took journeys together, and then wrote everything up. In every form of art – poetry, portraiture, sculpture, theatre, essays, fiction, journalism – there was an intense interest in expressing and analysing selfhood. 'The proper study of mankind is man', Pope wrote in *The Essay on Man* in 1733. At the other end of the century, Rousseau's posthumous *Confessions* (published between 1781 and 1788) promised the display, with hitherto unrivalled frankness, of a unique, incomparable individual. From Fielding and Defoe to Jane Austen and Fanny Burney, fictional personages were represented as individuals vividly marked by particular character traits, exploring life and seeking satisfaction through their relationships with other people. The products and processes of the book trade were closely bound up with this interest in personality and character. Literary correspondence was being published (starting with Pope's letters), autobiographies were being written, journals were being kept, in bulk.

Boswell's annotation of Johnson's life was not unique. The literary disciple following the great man around and taking down everything he says has stayed with us as an almost parodic image of biography. (Boswell was unfairly caricatured for having taken notes in company while Johnson was talking: in fact, he relied more on a good memory and quick writing-up after the event – if he left it too long, it was like 'pickling long-kept and faded fruits' – and he congratulates himself on having become better at 'taking down' Johnson as he grew less in awe of him.) But the practice of collecting and publishing the 'ana' (sayings) or 'anecdotes' of famous wise men went back a long way. You might call Plato's books Socratiana, or the New Testament, Messiana. Lives in the 17th century made great use of 'sayings'. The lawyer and orientalist John Selden's 'table talk' was collected by his secretary and published in 1689. French literary history of the 18th century was crowded with collections of 'ana'. Such collections showed an intense interest in great men's spoken words.

Women were not such objects of interest. There were plenty of women writers producing poems, plays, novels, diaries, letters, travel writings, essays, and hymns in the late 17th and early 18th centuries. But memoirs or 'ana' of women were not being collected. Instead, Margaret Cavendish, Duchess of Newcastle, wrote a life of her (living) husband, William Cavendish, in 1667, praising him to the skies for his virtues. (The panegyric was mocked by Pepys, who thought her 'a mad, conceited, ridiculous woman, and he an ass to suffer her to write what she writes'.) Lucy Hutchinson wrote a self-effacing, loving memoir of her husband Colonel Hutchinson, the Protestant regicide, in 1664, referring to herself throughout in the third person and extolling him as a Protestant saint: 'His life was nothing else but a progress from one degree of vertue to another.' The 19th-century novelist and autobiographer Margaret Oliphant said of it, in 1882: 'There is never an "I" in the book from beginning to end.' Hester Thrale wrote *Anecdotes of the Life of the late Samuel Johnson* in 1786. Fanny Burney edited her father's *Memoirs*.

The 'Great Men' whose sayings were being written down by their admirers were often writers, painters, or actors. There was a deep interest in imagination and creativity, in the life of the mind. The literary Oxford clergyman Joseph Spence met Pope in the mid-1720s and noted down his sayings from 1727 until Pope's death in 1744. Spence's 'Popeana' or *Anecdotes* circulated in manuscript for many years. Johnson saw the manuscript in 1780, when he was writing his Life of Pope. Spence provided materials for biography: he never wrote his own Life of Pope, and his manuscript was not published until 1820 (nor fully edited until the 1960s). The fashion for 'ana' continued, linking the centuries: there were William Seward's *Anecdotes of Some Distinguished Persons* (1795) and John Nichols' nine-volume *Literary Anecdotes of the Eighteenth Century*

(1812–16). In the 1820s and 1830s, soon after Spence's *Anecdotes* were published, Hazlitt published his *Conversations with Sir James Northcote* (the portrait-painter who had been Reynolds's pupil and friend), Fanny Burney's anecdotal *Memoirs* of her father Dr Burney came out, and Drummond's *Conversations with Ben Jonson*, dating from 1618, were published. Speech acts were valued. Conversation was a vital part of life, an art, a form of entertainment, and – in Johnson's case – a brow-beating competition. But Boswell was unusual in turning 'ana' into a whole biographical narrative, while keeping the fragmentary quality of an anthology. He was pioneering, too, as one of the first to publish private conversations so fully and candidly, and he got into trouble for it. Critics, of both the *Tour* and the *Life*, objected to his having exhibited all Johnson's 'unhappy infirmities', thereby 'disgracing a character . . . as wens and warts would do a statue or Portrait'.

The main ingredients of that scene on Skye, from the *Tour*, are all there in the *Life*. Boswell insists on his kind of biographical writing as a 'copartnership'. He takes pride in his own role. He stage-manages his main performer. He venerates, but is also wary of, his subject. He believes in conversation as the best way of 'displaying' character. He feels that the relationship he had with Johnson, which 'opened the spring' of that conversation, is of great value to himself and to the world. He is determined to write the truest version. 'Authenticity is my chief boast', he said of the *Tour* in 1785, to Edmond Malone, the Shakespeare scholar who gave him so much help and encouragement. In his 'Preface' and 'Advertisement' to the *Life* (addressed to Malone), Boswell used a cluster of words that are keys to his work, and to this phase of British biography: 'conversation', 'authenticity', 'fidelity', 'accuracy', 'intimately'. He believed – as Johnson did – that the point of life-writing was to be truthful and realistic: 'veracity' was one of their favourite words. Fidelity to the subject should not be a process of loyal concealment, but of accurate characterization. It was the 'minute particulars' that gave biography its usefulness.

'Authenticity', in the best sense, implied a moral standard, and a reaction against more dutiful or pious forms of life-writing. This reaction had set in well before Boswell. The lawyer and biographer Roger North, in a prescient unpublished manuscript dating from the 1730s, outlined all the arguments that would become familiar in the next two centuries, about the benefits of 'private lives' over public histories, the usefulness of ordinary men's life-stories, and the need for 'honesty' in biography. Johnson (who had not read North) made his own case for 'authenticity' long before he wrote most of his *Lives of the Poets*. His principles were set out, with typical confidence, in a famous essay written for his own magazine, the *Rambler*, in 1750. It claims that biography is the most 'delightful and useful' form of writing because 'the narrative of the lives of particular persons' allows us to sympathize with others. The 'judicious and faithful' story of almost any life is 'useful' because 'there is such a uniformity in the state of man', and we can recognize our own 'motives' and passions in the lives of others. Biographers need to choose the most important anecdotes to illustrate 'the manners and behaviour of their heroes'. Preferably, biography should be written from 'personal knowledge', but should not be dressed up with 'panegyrick'. 'If we owe regard to the memory of the dead, there is yet more respect to be paid to knowledge, to virtue, and to truth.' In a later essay in his magazine the *Idler*, Johnson argued that the most truthful life-writing is when 'the writer tells his own story', since only he knows the whole truth about himself. (He does not use the word 'autobiography', which only came into circulation in the early 19th century.) Those who write about another may want to over-praise him or 'aggravate his infamy'; those who write about themselves, he says – optimistically – have no 'motive to falsehood' except 'self-love', and we are all on the watch for that.

When Johnson wrote these essays he had already published, in his thirties, an extraordinarily pioneering *Life of Mr Richard Savage* (1744), the erratic poet and playwright, close friend of his twenties, whose struggles to survive in Grub Street included a criminal trial and an early death in the debtors' prison. Johnson's youthful sympathy for his strange friend inspired a fine book by Richard Holmes, which argues that the Life of Savage created a new, hybrid, 'romantic' non-fictional form, combining drama, romance, folk ballad, journalism, and morality. Writing it certainly crystallized Johnson's views on biography's ideal 'blend of sympathetic engagement and instructive detachment'. But Johnson's later *Lives of the Poets* were different. They were written, more than thirty years after the Life of Savage, not out of personal sympathy, but as commissioned prefaces to a new edition of 'the most eminent English poets', meant to analyse and place their works. Their main interest is in what makes a 'Genius' (especially in the Lives of Dryden and Pope). In the moral, realistic tradition of Plutarch, the *Lives* show off the 'usefulness' of anecdotes, a resistance to 'the mist of panegyric', powerful, strenuous, sometimes wilful critical attentiveness, and a clear sense of what can and can't be known about another person: 'Actions are visible, though motives are secret.' However, for all his earlier arguments that the value of biography is in the imaginative sympathy it can produce, Johnson's *Lives* can be ironic, opinionated, or brutally hostile, especially when he disapproves of a poet's politics:

Biography

> Milton's republicanism was, I am afraid, founded in an envious hatred of greatness, and a sullen desire of independence; in petulance impatient of controul, and pride disdainful of superiority . . . He hated all whom he was required to obey.

Johnson's strong, principled, argumentative voice spoke out of an often ruthless and opportunistic literary culture. The use of the word 'authentic' might be a cheap form of advertisement or a warning-sign of predators at work, rather than an indication of high moral value. As early as 1716, the essayist Joseph Addison was complaining about 'Grub-street biographers' as vultures, 'who watch for the death of a great man, like so many undertakers, on purpose to make a penny of him.' The most notorious of these grave-robbers was the book dealer Edmund Curll, Pope's lifelong enemy and butt, notorious for his piratic literary thefts, his pornography, his unauthorized editions of writers' letters, and his quick, cheap, cobbled-together biographies, which led to his being famously described, in the 1730s, as 'one of the new terrors of Death'. Curll's shamelessly exploitative publications would always be prefaced with the words 'Genuine' and 'Authentic', as in his 1745 *Life of Pope*, rushed out after his old enemy's death, 'Faithfully Collected From Authentic Authors, Original Manuscripts, and the Testimonies of many Persons of Credit and Honour'.

There were dangers in authenticity. To some readers – and in some hands – it meant betrayal, not fidelity. Boswell venerated his subject and wanted to do well by him, but he was also trying to make his mark in a self-advertising literary world. So – as always in the history of biography – Boswell's *Life* involved both low and high motives. And, like all memorable biographies, it mixed together many different genres and approaches.

It is vividly visual, showing us the physical Johnson in every light and at every angle, often unflatteringly. 'I am so nice in recording him' (Boswell wrote in his Journal) 'that every trifle must be authentic. I draw him in the style of a Flemish painter. I am not satisfied with hitting the large features. I must be exact as to every hair, or even every spot on his countenance.' What this 'Flemish picture' provides is 'a sustained act of looking' (which owes as much to Hogarth and to Reynolds as to the Dutch painters). Once Johnson's huge, odd body has been sighted in its 'uncouth', 'slovenly' badly fitting clothes, we keep seeing it in our mind's eye: his convulsive tics, his savage, sweating eating habits, his obsessive-compulsive habits of counting steps and shaking his body and rubbing his left knee, the way he 'scraped the joints of his fingers with a pen-knife, till they seemed quite red and raw'.

We see him and we hear him; he comes on stage and talks like an actor in a play, with Boswell as stage-manager. Their friend the actor David Garrick is one of the most important figures in the biography, and the *Life* is as theatrical as it is painterly, arranged in scenes set up to display Johnson's character. We seem to hear his voice in our ear, pontificating and pronouncing like Humpty Dumpty, whether on remarriage ('Johnson said it was the triumph of hope over experience') or on a leg of mutton: 'It is as bad as bad can be: it is ill-fed, ill-killed, ill-kept, and ill-drest'. We hear the strange sounds he makes when he is not actually talking, as if he is 'chewing the cud' or 'clucking like a hen' or – victorious over his opponent in conversation – blowing 'out his breath like a Whale'.

This pictorial drama also reads like a realist novel of its time. It keeps opening out into the surrounding texture of urban society, politics, manners, and domestic scenes, and provides a running commentary on the literary, theatrical, legal, artistic, and journalistic professions. Boswell's eager, proprietary attempts to get Johnson going, his inexhaustible curiosity in 'soliciting particulars' of Johnson's life, his fixing up of encounters which will produce the best Johnsonianisms, his rebuffs when Johnson rounds on him ('Don't you know that it is very uncivil to *pit* two people against one another?'), or sulks in his corner like the 'bear' he is often compared to, are funny. Part of the comedy is that Boswell knows how ridiculous he is. 'I know not how so whimsical a thought came into my mind, but I asked, "If, Sir, you were shut up in a castle, and a newborn child with you, what would you do?"' (Leslie Stephen, in his own *Life of Johnson* of 1879, called this 'exquisitely ludicrous': 'But a man capable of preferring such a remark to silence helps at any rate to keep the ball rolling.') The famous scene of 1776 in which Boswell manipulates Johnson into meeting the radical political writer John Wilkes, in the hopes of a conflagration, only to find Johnson treating Wilkes with humorous civility, is a fine example of the wit and brio (and the careful structuring) of Boswell's 'novel', and of his chameleon-like ability to echo and imitate Johnson: 'If I had come upon him with a direct proposal, "Sir, will you dine in company with Jack Wilkes?" he would have flown into a passion, and would probably have answered, "Dine with Jack Wilkes, Sir! I'd as soon dine with Jack Ketch." '

But there is more to this relationship than comedy, and part of the interest is that we want to see how the asexual but tender attachment between the biographer and his subject develops. Boswell's own depressions and anxieties, his veneration for Johnson as an alternative to his own disapproving father, and Johnson's ability to teach and advise him, make an affecting story: as when Boswell fusses over a small domestic problem, and Johnson 'laughed, and said, "Consider, Sir, how insignificant this will appear a twelvemonth hence" '. Though Boswell insists that he is following Johnson's example in not giving us 'panegyrick', he also wants to 'infuse every drop of genuine sweetness into [his] biographical cup', citing others to show how 'few persons quitted his company without perceiving themselves wiser and better than they were before', and insisting that Johnson could be 'civil, obliging, nay, polite' as often as he could be 'violent', 'with a club in his hand, to knock down everyone who approached him'. ' "Well, (said he), we had good talk." BOSWELL: "Yes, Sir; you tossed and gored several persons." ' He takes care to contrast, with all the conversational tossing and goring, moments when Johnson shows a wistful, tender, affectionate side, as when, talking of a young man who is 'running about town shooting cats', Johnson 'in a sort of kindly reverie ... bethought himself of his own favourite cat, and said, "But Hodge shan't be shot; no, no, Hodge shall not be shot." '

Boswell's Johnson is the man of letters as epic hero (as well as comic grotesque), and it is one of the new features of this late 18th-century biography that secular, bourgeois, everyday life should be the vehicle for heroic qualities. The heroism lies in Johnson's commitment to truth, his endurance, his philosophic stoicism wrestling with his dark, lonely, troubled, passionate mind, his struggle with the fear of death: 'So much so, Sir, that the whole of life is but keeping away the thoughts of it.' When Boswell compares

Johnson's mind to the Coliseum at Rome, with his judgement at the centre like a 'mighty gladiator' doing battle with the 'apprehensions' that assail him like 'wild beasts', he makes his rationalist secular hero into a Christian martyr. This is not a saint's life, but Boswell gives Johnson spiritual victories, disciples, intellectual influence, and a good death.

The Life mixes genres, and it also mixes ways of thinking about the self. Johnson and Boswell both believe in the usefulness of biography in displaying moral values. In that sense they continue the exemplary tradition in life-writing derived from Plutarch and from Christian hagiography. But the presentation of identity in the Life is complicated, subtle, and new. There are at least two kinds of selfhood on display, two lines of behaviour. Broadly speaking, one line derives from Pope, Johnson's hero, and the other from Rousseau, whose novels Boswell much admired when he was young, and whom Johnson detested. The kind of behaviour on show that links to Rousseau is sentimental, tender, tearful, and confessional – as when, 'such was his sensibility', Johnson weeps when reading poetry. The line that can be associated with Pope is robust, satirical, observant, stoic: 'He advised me . . . when I was moving about, to read diligently the great book of mankind.' 'Let us endeavour to see things as they are', Johnson writes to a friend in 1758, 'and then enquire whether we ought to complain.'

That complex sense of what personality consists of will have a profound effect on biographical writing. Johnson is not a fixed entity, and nor is his biographer. In the dance of conversation and copartnership between the two, the figures seem to move about, talk, and think in front of us, embodied and immediate, though so long vanished into the past – as here, when Boswell, about to leave England for Utrecht, is saying goodbye to Johnson at Harwich:

> My revered friend walked down with me to the beach, where we embraced and parted with tenderness, and engaged to correspond

by letters. I said, 'I hope, Sir, you will not forget me in my absence.' JOHNSON: 'Nay, Sir, it is more likely you should forget me, than that I should forget you.' As the vessel put out to sea, I kept my eyes upon him for a considerable time, while he remained rolling his majestick frame in his usual manner: and at last I perceived him walk back into the town, and he disappeared.

Chapter 4
National Biography

Conversation, friendship, collaboration, quarrels; letters telling of personal feelings and encounters, of work in progress and political opinions; confessional narratives of addiction, love, and weakness; journals of domestic life; manuscripts circulating between small groups: early 19th-century literature was criss-crossed with a spider's web of life-writing. 'Self-fashioning' took many forms. In Europe, Rousseau's confessional individualism and his linking of natural passion and virtue, Goethe's 'elective affinities' transcending social laws, Herder's philosophy of self-defining subjectivity, profoundly influenced the telling of life-stories. In America, the intellectual declarations of independence of Transcendentalist thinkers like Emerson and Thoreau insisted on 'self-reliance' and a connection to nature for the forging of a true identity. Self-expression ran through every literary genre. Biography, character-sketches, autobiography, memoirs, diaries, travel-writing, and correspondence overlapped. For the British Romantic writers there was a porous line between published work (often scandalously autobiographical, even if written in disguise) and private writings passed between friends. Interior lives were closely bound up with group relations. Writers described each other, worked and lived together (sometimes catastrophically), published and reviewed each other, agonized over the survival and publication of personal documents, and looked anxiously for the right biographers to do justice to the dead.

The emphasis in life-writing was on empathy. William Hazlitt called his 1820s *Conversations* with the old portrait-painter James Northcote 'Boswell Redivivus', but he was more impressionistic than Boswell: 'My object was to catch the tone and manner, rather than to repeat the exact expressions, or even opinions.' Coleridge thought that too much 'minutiae' in a biography or memoir could 'render the real character almost invisible, like clouds of dust on a portrait'. The first British book on biography, written by James Stansfield in 1813, argued for a mixture of 'sympathetic emotion', 'impartiality', and 'moral illustration' – and for censoring 'particulars' which 'do not reflect great honour on the deceased'.

But life-writing also involved gossip, gusto, satire, and comedy. Romantic biography had teeth. Descriptions, for example, of Coleridge's extraordinary conversational manner show how wicked such writings could be. Hazlitt (who met Coleridge in 1798, and wrote about him with mixed admiration and disappointment in the early 1820s) described a 'tangential' mind which spilt itself in talking: 'If Mr Coleridge had not been the most impressive talker of his age, he would probably have been the finest writer . . . he may be said to have lived on the sound of his own voice.' Thomas Carlyle, who saw Coleridge in old age, wrote a lethal description in the 1850s of his 'confused unintelligible flood of utterance, threatening to submerge all known landmarks of thought', his habit of corkscrewing from one side of the garden path to the other ('he never could fix which side would suit him best'), and his plaintive, snuffling, sing-song voice: ' "Ah, your tea is too cold, Mr Coleridge!" mourned the good Mrs Gilman once . . . handing him a very tolerable though belated cup. "It's better than I deserve!" snuffled he, in a low hoarse murmur, partly courteous, chiefly pious, the tone of which still abides with me: "It's better than I deserve!" '

That anecdotal sharpness, one of the vital qualities of biography, was fuelled by a dislike of Coleridge's hazy idealism. There were ideological wars going on in early 19th-century biography, reflecting – as biography always does – the politics of the time. Life-writing could be boldly radical. Hazlitt's commitment to civil liberties energized his character-sketches of politicians and poets in *The Spirit of the Age* (1825) and his editing of the *Memoirs* of the working-class Jacobin writer Thomas Holcroft. William Godwin's short biography of his wife Mary Wollstonecraft, published in 1798, soon after her death in childbirth, as *Memoirs of the Author of 'The Rights of Woman'*, caused outrage for its candid account of her feminism, atheism, and anti-establishment views. Biography of this sort was dangerous, and would produce a backlash of censoriousness.

But sympathy was the key for Godwin as, fifty years on, for Carlyle, in his late Romantic biography of 1851 of 'a brilliant human presence', the unsuccessful poet John Sterling, who died young in 1844. Unlike Carlyle's later epic, historical biography of Frederick the Great, this is biography as confession, brimful with elegiac melancholy for 'this most friendly, bright and beautiful human soul; who walked with me for a season in this world, and remains to me very memorable while I continue in it'. When Boswell's *Life of Johnson* was republished in the 1830s, Carlyle wrote about biography as a sacred enterprise.

> In Boswell's 'Life of Johnson', how indelibly and magically bright does many a little Reality dwell in our remembrance! ... some slight, perhaps mean and even ugly incident, if *real* and well-presented, will fix itself in a susceptive memory, and lie ennobled there ... with the pathos which belongs only to the Dead. For the Past is all holy to us; the Dead are all holy, even they that were base, and wicked while alive ...

He instances the glimpse of Boswell and Johnson walking along the Strand arm-in-arm at night, and being accosted by a 'woman of the town':

Strange power of Reality! Not even this poorest of occurrences, but now, after seventy years are come and gone, has a meaning for us. Do but consider that it is *true*; that it did in very deed occur! ... Johnson said, 'No, no, my girl; it won't do'; and then 'we talked'; – and herewith the wretched one, seen but for the twinkling of an eye, passes on into the utter Darkness.

How, he asks, can biography do this – invoke such 'light-gleams' of reality?

One grand, invaluable secret there is ... : *To have an open loving heart, and what follows from the possession of such* ... This is it that opens the whole mind, quickens every faculty of the intellect to do its fit work, that of *knowing*; and therefrom, by sure consequence, of *vividly uttering-forth.*

It is one of the great justifications of biography as a humane discipline – and it is very much of its time. If asked what the key to biographical success is now, we probably would not reply: 'to have an open loving heart'. And 'a loving heart' is a risky basis for life-writing. The impulses of sympathy and veneration that dominated much 19th-century biography often solidified into hagiography. Though many different kinds of Lives were being written between the 1830s and the 1890s, the period has come to be retrospectively caricatured for white-washing and censorship. The hallmarks of Victorian biography – quite unlike the risky narratives of the generation before – were morality and reticence. Carlyle saw this coming, reviewing the critic John Gibson Lockhart's 1837 *Memoirs* of his father-in-law, Walter Scott, which was causing outrage for exposing the 'sanctities of private life'.

How delicate, decent is English biography, bless its mealy mouth! A Damocles' sword of *Respectability* hangs for ever over the poor English life-writer (as it does over poor English life in general) and reduces him to the verge of paralysis.

But discretion increasingly became the norm, in a period when class-consciousness, religious belief, social aspirations, serious evangelical moral standards, work ethic, fears of European-style revolution, and national loyalties, were such central themes in fiction and poetry – and in everyday middle-class life. Literary remains and reputations were being tidied up, as in the apologetic tone of Lockhart's 1828 biography of Burns (excusing the poet's 'dissipation' by pointing to 'the moral influence of his genius'), or the burning of Byron's scandalous journals in his publisher's office in 1824, or the Shelley family's efforts to sanctify his posthumous life. When the real stories of dead poets' intense emotions burst through these safeguards, as with Shelley's shocking 'irregular relations', scorching the pages of a guarded, compromised 1888 biography by Edward Dowden, or the publication in 1878 of Keats's love-letters to Fanny Brawne, there was always an outcry.

Biography in the mid to late 19th century was often written by a descendant or a disciple. The essential materials – letters, diaries, secrets – were usually in the family's possession. If the biographer was commissioned by the family, he (or, much less often, she) could only read what was given out, and had to be careful not to cause offence. There were many examples of protective Lives written by friends or family. These included Arthur Penrhyn Stanley's 1844 Life of Dr Thomas Arnold, the headmaster of Rugby who had been his teacher; John Forster's of his revered friend Charles Dickens (1872–4); G. O. Trevelyan's of his uncle Macaulay (1876); and Hallam Tennyson's of his father, the Poet Laureate (1897), written under the censoring eye of his mother Emily Tennyson. Widows of famous men such as Charles Kingsley piously memorialized their late husbands. Family biographers were well aware of their compromised position: Leslie Stephen, setting out gloomily to write a dutiful, commissioned life of his older brother, the legislator James Fitzjames Stephen, whom he had always found unsympathetic, asked himself: what 'if Boswell had been Johnson's brother?' His daughter Virginia Woolf would satirize the writing of such family biography in her 1919 novel *Night and Day*, part of a whole literary generation's scathing reaction against Victorian Lives.

Yet there was a great deal to be said for affectionate, venerating biography. Forster's *Dickens* was censored and inaccurate, but it also gave a sympathetic, energetic close-up of its remarkable subject. Elizabeth Gaskell's Life of her fellow novelist Charlotte Brontë told a tender and moving story. Gaskell had few precedents in 1857 for the writing of a woman's life by a woman. She was six years older than her subject and admired her work. They met in 1850, when Gaskell was forty; she had recently published *Mary Barton*; Brontë, *Jane Eyre*. After Brontë's death in 1855 at the age of thirty-eight, Gaskell was asked by the Reverend Patrick Brontë (who had outlived all his children) to write the Life. She approached her subject with sympathy and respect, as an equal – and also as a woman with her own history of family bereavements. Brontë had lost her mother and all her siblings; Gaskell's parents had died when she was young and she had lost two children. Her approach was protective: she wanted to defend Brontë against the accusations of immorality and coarseness which had greeted *Jane Eyre*, and she did so by suppressing her knowledge of Brontë's passionate love-letters to the married M. Heger in Brussels, and by emphasizing her femininity and religious stoicism over her professional achievements.

Gaskell noted down three suggestive quotations to guide her. One read: 'If you love your reader and want to be read, get anecdotes!' One spoke of the need for a 'tender tie' between biographer and subject. And one, from a friend of Brontë's, noted her 'boundless sphere of feeling and intellect crammed into a silent existence'. Gaskell set out to write a narrative of tragic loss, loneliness, anguish, Christian fortitude, and 'dignified endurance', set with novelistic vividness in the dark, gloomy Yorkshire moorland setting of Haworth. Small domestic details of Brontë's life as a daughter and sister dominate the story. One eloquent example is the story of Charlotte's interrupting her writing of *Jane Eyre* to cut

a

b

9. Charlotte Brontë and Elizabeth Gaskell: Two women, two friends, two novelists: biography as the art of sympathy

out the eyes in the potatoes which Tabby, the housekeeper, was too old and blind to see.

> Miss Brontë was too dainty a housekeeper to put up with this; yet she could not bear to hurt the faithful old servant ... Accordingly she would steal into the kitchen, and quietly carry off the bowl of vegetables ... and breaking off in the full flow of interest and inspiration in her writing, carefully cut out the specks in the potatoes, and noiselessly carry them back to their place. This little proceeding may show how orderly and fully she accomplished her duties, even at those times when the 'possession' was upon her.

The very next paragraph begins with an account of the 'singular felicity' in Brontë's choice of words in her writing, as though precision and fastidiousness in writing and housekeeping go alongside each other, even though they may conflict.

When Gaskell describes her subject as an author rather than a private person, it is, specifically, as a woman author:

> When a man becomes an author, it is probably merely a change of employment to him. He takes a portion of that time which has hitherto been devoted to some other study or pursuit; he gives up something of the legal or medical profession ... or relinquishes part of the trade or business by which he has been striving to gain a livelihood; and another merchant or lawyer, or doctor, steps into his place ... But no other can take up the quiet, regular duties of the daughter, the wife, or the mother, as well as she whom God has appointed to fill that particular place: a woman's principal work in life is hardly left to her own choice ... And yet she must not shrink from the extra responsibility implied by the very fact of her possessing [the most splendid talents that ever were bestowed]. She must not hide her gift in a napkin; it was meant for the use and service of others.

Later biographers of Charlotte Brontë have reproached Gaskell for (as Carolyn Heilbrun put it) restoring her 'to the safety of womanliness', and for promoting 'the myth of her unswerving faith'. But Gaskell's admirers have warmed to the biography's novelistic empathy and generosity. Margaret Oliphant called it a new kind of biography, a plea 'for every woman dropped out of sight'. Christopher Ricks thinks it 'the greatest life of a woman by a woman'. Gaskell's biographer, Jenny Uglow, says that 'with all its silences, large and small, *The Life of Charlotte Brontë* is profoundly expressive'.

Victorian biographies could be eloquent and vivid. And though respect and reticence shadowed them, quirks of temperament, oddity, and strangeness lurked in the margins. 'Eccentric Biography' was, indeed, a thriving popular genre all through the 19th century. Memoirs, group biographies, pamphlets, and 'Wonderful Magazines' told uncensored life-stories of the very odd. Henry Wilson's collection of *Wonderful Characters*, first published in 1821, was still going strong in the 1870s. Frederick Fairholt's *Remarkable Characters* (1849), John Timbs's *English Eccentrics and Eccentricities* (1866), William Russell's two-volume *Eccentric Personages* (1864), and Robert Malcolm's *Curiosities of Biography* (1865) were just as popular. There were collections of freaks, misers, clerical and medical eccentrics, remarkable females, and regional curiosities (*Three Wonderful Yorkshire Characters*). Timbs categorized his English Eccentrics under 'wealth and fashion, delusions, impostures and fanatic missions, hermits, fat people, giants, dwarfs and strong men...eccentric travellers, artists, theatrical people, and men of letters'. The eccentrics who did not fit into any of these categories had to go under 'miscellaneous'.

All the same, in mainstream biography, there was a generally stolid air to the 'Lives and Letters' of the period. They followed a formula of a lengthy chronological narrative, often, like the novels of the time, in several volumes, with extensive (but tactfully censored) extracts from letters and diaries. The stories told were of public achievement, professional challenges, friendships, travel, battles, political dilemmas, or crises of faith. Childhood problems, domestic privacies, affairs, and scandals were played down. The main characters were politicians and statesmen, military or naval heroes, churchmen, writers, and teachers. The trajectory led upwards and onwards, the tone was generally serious and uncritical. John Cross, George Eliot's widower, published a Life in 1885 of such decorousness that Gladstone complained: 'It is not a Life at all ... It is a Reticence in three volumes.' Gladstone himself was venerated in a Life by his friend John Morley (1903), culminating, as Victorian biography often did, in a good death in the bosom of the family, which passed over (at the daughter's request) the horrible details of Gladstone's mouth cancer, and substituted a last page as from a Victorian novel:

> On the early morning of the 19th [May 1898], his family all kneeling around the bed on which he lay in the stupor of coming death, without a struggle he ceased to breathe. Nature outside – wood and wide lawn and cloudless far-off sky – shone at her fairest.

That sort of hagiography would be mocked by the next generation, as much for its ideology as for its prose style. But there were strong reasons for such biographical hero-worship. Biography is never just the personal story of one life. It always has political and social implications. The politics of 19th-century biography had to do with consolidating a national story. In North America, a distinctive national culture was being forged between the wars of Independence and the Civil War; in Europe, national identities were re-shaping themselves through a period of immense turbulence. In Britain, at the start of the century, great social changes, fears of unrest, political repression after the Napoleonic Wars, led to an investment in heroic Lives as a form of security. Later, they became expressions of imperial confidence and assertiveness. A biography which famously set the tone for life-writing as a form of patriotism was Robert Southey's *Life of Nelson* (1813), which excused all his personal weaknesses in order to immortalize 'a name and an example, which are at this hour inspiring thousands of the youth of England; a name which is our pride, and an example which will continue to be our strength and shield'.

But you did not have to be Nelson in order to contribute to the national story, and you did not have to be the subject of a three-volume Life in order to be remembered. In Europe and America, all through the 19th century, biographical dictionaries were being compiled of all those thought worthy of memorialization. Belknap's collective *American Biography* came out in the 1790s. In Europe, from the 1830s onwards, there were multi-volume dictionaries of illustrious Italians, Swedes, Dutch, Belgians, Austrians, and Germans. In France, Louis-Gabriel Michaud's 52-volume *Biographie Universelle Ancienne et Moderne*, published between 1811 and 1828, covered all kinds of public figures and spawned numerous French imitators, all aiming to create a universal national narrative out of individual life-stories.

In Britain, the National Portrait Gallery was founded in 1856, with a historical, patriotic agenda summed up by one of the great Victorian portrait-painters, G. F. Watts: 'The character of a nation as a people of great deeds is one … that should never be lost sight of.' Portraits – and, later, photographs – of British people of note made a visual biographical collection of, and for, the nation. The equivalent in print took longer to establish. Since Thomas Fuller's *Worthies of England* in 1662, and big biographical dictionaries like the multi-volume *Biographia Brittanica* (1747–66), there had been many collections of short biographies of worthy – or scandalous – lives, organized by county, region, type, or profession. In the mid-19th century, there were collections of 'Eminent and Illustrious Englishmen', 'Eminent English Judges', 'Famous Indian Chiefs', 'Notorious and Daring Highwaymen', 'Some of the More Celebrated Jewish Rabbis', 'Sundry Notorious Villains', 'Lives of Good Servants', admirals, apostles, bachelor kings, bigamists, bishops, martyrs, physicians, prophets, rakes, and regicides. 'Lives of Illustrious Shoemakers' (1883) told, for instance, the story of

'Samuel Drew: The Metaphysical Shoemaker', 'the self-taught Cornishman plying his lonely craft while he lays the foundation for his fame as a theologian'. Women featured in these collections as saints, poetesses, servants, criminals, and queens, under titles such as 'Stories of the Lives of Noble Women' or 'Memoirs of Several Ladies of Great Britain, who have been Celebrated for their Writings'. A collection called 'English Female Worthies', by Mrs John Sandford, published in 1883, consisting of hagiographies of Protestant 'saints' such as Lady Jane Grey, shows what terms were required for writing 'female biography':

> It is not to be expected that the lives of women should, in general, exhibit any peculiar striking incidents, or afford material for very animated narrative. Confined as the sex, for the most part, are to private life, they are not often participators in the stirring scenes which mark the period in which they live ... Female biography, therefore, does not owe its chief interest to the events which it records ... The quiet days of a woman usually present little more than a succession of private duties, or the ordinary events of domestic life ... Yet may they not be the less worthy of notice on that account. To trace the development of character is the chief end in all biography.

The most famous – and best-selling – of these educational, nationalistic publications were Samuel Smiles' male-dominated *Self-Help* (1859) and *Lives of The Engineers* (1861–2), celebrations of the work and energy of the 'lesser-known' as heroic contributions to 'our power as a nation'. One example out of hundreds gives the tone: the story of William Jackson of Birkenhead ('the present member for North Derbyshire'), the seventh of eleven children, whose father died when he was little, who was put to work on the docks and then in the counting-house, and who, 'having obtained access to a set of the *Encyclopaedia Britannica*, read the volumes through from A to Z, partly by day, but chiefly by night. He afterwards put himself to a trade, was diligent, and succeeded in it. Now . . . he holds commercial relations with nearly every country on the globe.'

Smiles was part of educational movements such as the *Society for the Diffusion of Useful Knowledge*, which aimed to encourage self-help for the workers through education rather than revolution. His, and similar inspirational secular stories, were 'designed to be to the early machine age what collections of saints' legends had been to the Middle Ages'. There was a polemical agenda, also, behind popular late 19th-century series of cultural figures and national leaders like John Morley's *English Men of Letters* (from 1877), his *Twelve English Statesmen* (from 1888), and George Grove's *Dictionary of Music and Musicians* (from 1879).

In 1885, after many years of discussion on the need for a British equivalent to the *Biographie Universelle*, the *Dictionary of National Biography*, published by George Smith and edited by Leslie Stephen (and then by Sidney Lee, after Stephen gave up from strain and overwork), started its long history of publication. The first edition – containing the lives of almost 29,000 dead British people – was completed, in 63 volumes, in 1900, with three supplements in 1901. Supplements and revisions continued all through the 20th century until, in 1992, work began on a new, hugely expanded and thoroughly revised DNB, published as the *Oxford Dictionary of National Biography* in 2004.

Leslie Stephen set out to provide, in what he called (in imitation of the 18th-century prototype) his 'Biographia Britannica', 'the greatest possible amount of information in a thoroughly business-like form'. The entries had to be 'strictly biographical', factual, not 'overcrowded' with detail, impersonal but not hostile, 'written by persons who sympathize with the subject'. Grounds for inclusion in this collective national history were democratic and secular. The great names were all there, but also those whom Leslie Stephen called minor heroes: naval captains, country vicars, teachers, merchants, sportsmen. These were lives which had to be reconstructed from obituaries, memoirs, prefaces, letters, and 'who really become generally accessible through the dictionary alone'. And there were more dubious characters too: 'brothel-keepers, contortionists, gamblers, transvestites and centenarians'. Women made up only 4% of the entries, since there were relatively few in public life, and wives and mothers featured as mere appendages.

Time changes our concept of who deserves to have their life-story preserved, their biography written. In 1993, almost a hundred years after the original DNB completed publication in 1900, a volume of *Missing Persons* was published (with 1,074 additional names from all periods). The editor, Christine Nicholls, prefaced it with a thoughtful commentary on the exclusions of her predecessors. She notes that in the period from the end of the 17th century to mid-Victorian Britain:

> there often went unnoticed by the original editors, perhaps
> reasonably, those whose achievements, not always conspicuous, by
> deeds and invention … provided the secure underpinning of a
> society in constant rapid change and expansion in population and
> possessions. Here we find explorers, chemists, aeronauts,
> hydrographers, shippers, royal servants, architects, sailors,
> inventors, doctors, and practical men and women more often than
> visionaries or poets, speculators rather than speculatives, hard
> sloggers rather than loud mouths – without whom the smooth
> modulation of changing national structures would have been lost.
> The passage of time was necessary to establish their claims.

From the 1850s to the mid-20th century, 'there appear large numbers of businessmen, engineers, scientists, and women – all categories which had suffered some neglect'.

Yet, for all its historical blindspots, the 19th-century DNB provided a different kind of biography from the 'Lives and Letters' of Great Men. After his wife died in 1895, Leslie Stephen wrote an emotional essay called 'Forgotten Benefactors', celebrating the far-reaching influence of 'thousands who have long sunk into oblivion'. This Victorian theme, often used as an excuse for keeping women in the home, also provided an alternative concept of heroism, and a justification for writing the biographies of 'obscure' lives. It is found, too, on the last page of George Eliot's *Middlemarch* (1871) where Dorothea's obscure yet remarkable life is given as an example of those whose 'unhistoric acts' have an 'incalculably diffusive' influence: 'and that things are not so ill with you and me as they might have been, is half owing to the number who lived faithfully a hidden life, and rest in unvisited tombs'.

The great nationalistic production of the DNB came out of a prolific and increasingly professionalized 19th-century biographical industry. And its publication coincided with an intense and widespread debate about the ethics of life-writing. This was particularly vociferous in France, where biography was often despised as a low form of cultural life, and arguments raged over the relative merits of biography and history. The philosopher Victor Cousin maintained that individual life-stories reduced history to 'undistinguished trivia'. In his influential *Vie de Jésus* (1863), which presented its subject not as the Son of God but as an exceptional human being, Ernest Renan felt the need to justify a biographical approach as the best way of understanding the development of Christianity. The rise of a mass media, and the popularity of the journalistic, often scandalous, 'biographie' of the living, was viewed by some as a democratic plague, lowering literary culture to the 'exhibition of personality' and 'the squalor of personal data'.

The same anxieties were felt in America and Britain, as journalistic intrusion, the beginnings of celebrity culture, and the ever more shaky dividing line between private and public, gave rise to debates uncannily like our own, over a hundred years on, about the exhibiting of private lives for mass consumption. Public figures (like Parnell) could be toppled by personal scandal. Famous writers were aghast at the exposure of other writers' lives. Browning imagined the front of a house ripped off for people to peer inside.

Tennyson laid a public curse on the 'carrion vulture' who waits to tear the poet's heart 'before the crowd', and said, privately, that 'the lives of great men' were being 'ripped open like pigs'. George Eliot called biography 'a disease of English literature'. Thackeray warned his daughters that 'When I drop there is to be no life of me, *mind* this.'

Henry James wrote with horrified brilliance, in *The Aspern Papers* (1888) and elsewhere, about the violation of the writer's secret life by 'publishing scoundrels'. He passionately believed that 'a man's table-drawers and pockets should not be turned inside out', burned many private papers in the (useless) hope of 'frustrating' biographical intrusion, and resented the posthumous 'exhibition' of friends such as Robert Louis Stevenson. The trial and disgrace of Oscar Wilde in 1895 gripped and appalled him: 'Yes' (he wrote to Edmund Gosse), 'it is hideously, atrociously dramatic & really interesting – so far as one can say that of a thing of which the interest is qualified by such a sickening horribility.' He was as fascinated by the private lives of writers as he was horrified by their exposure. When he went on a motor-tour of France in 1907 with Edith Wharton, for instance, he couldn't wait to visit George Sand's house in Nohant to see the rooms where George and her lovers had, as he put it, 'pigged so thrillingly together'. And he read biography, memoirs, and letters with excitement.

'Ransacking', 'violation', 'betrayal', 'reticence', were key terms in the debate about biographical intrusion. The 'ethics of biography' became the subject of solemn discussion, as in an 1883 essay by Margaret Oliphant, who argued that the 'high-minded' biographer had a duty of responsibility to 'the helplessness of the dead', whose 'private drawers' could so easily be 'ransacked for evidence to their disadvantage'. Biographical betrayal, she concluded, was 'an offence against social morals'.

Oliphant was referring to the most notorious 'biographical betrayal' of the time, that of Carlyle, the greatly venerated Victorian sage. In the 1870s, Carlyle gave his friend, the historian John Anthony Froude, most of his papers, including his remorseful 'Reminiscences' of his late wife, Jane Welsh Carlyle, and the letters between them, with instructions to Froude to publish as he thought fit and to write his biography after his death. Froude saw that these materials revealed a shocking story of an unhappy marriage, but felt he owed it to his mentor to be as much of a truth-teller as Carlyle was himself. After Carlyle died in 1881, Froude immediately published the *Reminiscences*, followed by a respectful, vigorous Life in two volumes (1882, 1884), and the painful *Letters and Memorials of Jane Welsh Carlyle* (1883). He justified these publications by appealing to Carlyle's own belief that 'in proportion to a man's greatness is the scrutiny to which his conduct is submitted'. Howls of nationwide execration resulted. Biographical controversies always require someone to be blamed, and Froude was blamed for 'staining' the great man's name with these revelations of domestic cruelty, for getting his facts wrong, and for making unauthorized use of private papers. 'Froudacity' became a byword for treachery, immorality, and inaccuracy. After his death, his heirs published *My Relations with Carlyle* (1903), which explained that he had concealed the true reason Carlyle was so 'ill to live with', and Jane so discontented: Carlyle was impotent, 'one of those persons who ought never to have married'. Renewed outrage followed, spreading into medical and legal discussions about virility, marriage, and divorce. 'The frank biography has its limits', fulminated one critic in the pages of the *British Medical Journal*, 'and has not hitherto been held to include the history of a man's sexual experiences. It has been reserved for Froude to set a most pernicious example and inflict a stain on English literature by proclaiming abroad a genital defect in the man whose life he has been commissioned to write, and whom he affects to hold up to admiration . . .'

Froude's *Carlyle* is a good example of how closely biography is always involved with the social preoccupations of its time – and of how dangerous to the biographer personal intimacy with the subject can prove. 'It is always Judas who writes the biography', said Oscar Wilde in 1891. Froude, who never meant or wanted to be Judas, played a part, almost in spite of himself, in a shift towards more openness and directness in biography. A self-consciousness was developing about the practice of the craft, an interest in biography's aesthetic rather than its ethical implications, question marks about the extent to which it could ever be true to the private, inner self of the subject. Carlyle, the hero of this chapter, had thought about all that. He wrote in his journal in 1843:

> The world has no business with my life. The world will never know of my life, if it should write and read a hundred biographies of me. The main facts of it are known, and are likely to be known, to myself alone of all created men.

Chapter 5
Fallen Idols

George Bernard Shaw joked, in 1881, that what was needed for biography was a book called 'Queen Victoria: By a Personal Acquaintance Who Dislikes Her'. Lytton Strachey picked up the hint in the 1900s. He and other young British writers, who were living through catastrophic historical upheavals and startling social changes, preferred Shaw, H. G. Wells, and Samuel Butler to Carlyle or Tennyson, pacifism to patriotism, frankness to decorum, laughter to solemnity, secularism to religion. They sweepingly denigrated Victorian biography as a 'clumsy and laborious' monstrosity, 'dominated by the idea of goodness'. Evelyn Waugh, for instance, wrote in 1928 of the two-volume eulogy meant 'to assist with our fathers' decorum at the lying-in-state of our great men', 'their faces serenely composed and cleansed of all the stains of humanity'. The children of those fathers set out to change the way life-stories could be written (and writing about fathers was part of the story). The 'art of biography' used miniaturism, craft and craftiness, imaginative fictional tactics, irony, parody, and caricature. 'The corpse', Waugh noted, 'has become the marionette.' The biographer could be the equal, not the respectful or awe-struck disciple, of the subject. Biographers were self-conscious; biography might even be seen as a form of autobiography. Above all, biography aimed to uncover the inner self behind the public figure, with the help of the new tool of psychoanalysis.

Cultural shifts get over-simplified. Biography in the 19th century ✓
was not as monolithic and stolid as its detractors have claimed;
biography at the start of the 20th century was not all candid,
psychoanalytical, and experimental. Plenty of protective, decorous
biographies went on being written, such as Edward Marsh's 1918
idealized memoir of the golden boy-poet Rupert Brooke, or Rupert
Hart-Davis's *Hugh Walpole*, which, as late as 1952, omitted his
homosexuality. But a surge of factors, great and small, local and
global – the Carlyle-Froude and Wilde scandals, the death of
Queen Victoria, suffrage campaigns, Freud, the War – all played
their part in the shake-up. What Virginia Woolf called 'the new
biography' had definable characteristics. They are on view, variously,
over a period of about forty years, in Walter Pater's *Marius the
Epicurean* (1885) and his *Imaginary Portraits* (1887); Marcel
Schwob's 1895 short lives, *Vies Imaginaires*; Edmund Gosse's
memoir *Father and Son* (1907), and his essays on biography; Lytton
Strachey's four short Lives of *Eminent Victorians* (1918), and, less
influentially, his *Queen Victoria* (1921) and *Elizabeth and Essex*
(1928); Geoffrey Scott's *Portrait of Zélide* (1925); Virginia Woolf's
essays on the art of biography, her fictional biographies, *Orlando*
(1928) and *Flush* (1933), and her unfinished memoir 'Sketch of the
Past' (1939–41); Harold Nicolson's *The Development of English
Biography* (1928) and his whimsical portraits, *Some People* (1927);
André Maurois' *Ariel: Ou La Vie de Shelley* (1923, translated 1924)
and his *Aspects de la Biographie* (1928, translated 1929); Arthur
Symons' experiment in biography, *The Quest for Corvo* (1934); and
Emil Ludwig's *Die Kunst der Biographie* (1936).

The word 'biography' is coming under pressure here. As for the
18th century, with its mixture of 'ana' and satires, journals and
conversations, 'life-writing' is a more useful term for this mixture
of auto/biographical memoirs, satiric sketches, fictionalized or
psychoanalytical quests, and investigations of how life-stories can
be written. Virginia Woolf used the term in 'Sketch of the Past',
talking about the need to place the individual life in the context of
family, inheritance, environment, and 'invisible presences', to put

10. Woolf and Strachey. Irony, playfulness, and style: the modernists' approach to biography

'the fish in the stream'. In order to do this, she argued, there had to be new approaches. The blurring or breaking down of genres was part of the rethinking of biography.

Edmund Gosse (not usually known for adventurousness) produced a wonderfully uncategorizable book in *Father and Son*, his poignant, funny memoir of a very odd childhood. It was a pioneering genre, not a biography of his parents, nor an autobiography, but 'a study of two temperaments'. Gosse's account of his upbringing in a group of fundamentalist Calvinist 'Brethren', by his widowed father, Philip Gosse, a naturalist caught between his scientific curiosity and his religious beliefs, exposed a private family life with more candour than readers were used to. Gosse treats his father's scrupulous struggle to bring up a small boy according to rigid principles as at once admirable and pitiful. There are comic, rueful scenes where the son begins to doubt the father's infallibility, like his experiment with an 'act of idolatry', praying to the morning-room chair ('O Chair!'), as a fearful test of God's wrath ('but nothing happened . . . God did not care'), or his 'spiritual anguish' at having secretly had a mouthful of forbidden plum pudding at Christmas: 'Oh! Papa, Papa, I have eaten of flesh offered to idols!'. *Father and Son* was praised for its truthfulness, and also blamed for 'going too far'. But it has had a long afterlife as a vivid, humane account of a father–son relationship, setting a standard for many later novelistic memoirs such as Philip Roth's *Patrimony*, or Blake Morrison's *And When Did You Last See Your Father?*

Striking the father dead was part of the agenda for Lytton Strachey. *Eminent Victorians* has rightly been described as 'Oedipal biography'. Strachey, a child of the Empire's governing classes, was a brilliant, mannered, gangling, sickly intellectual, passionate in his friendships, in love with French and 18th-century literature, fascinated by Freudian psychoanalysis, a witty homosexual 'character' in his Cambridge and Bloomsbury circle. Though he wrote history, 'portraits', and criticism throughout his rather short life (he died at fifty-two), he became famous – and would be mainly remembered – for one book. *Eminent Victorians* had a powerful effect, now hard to re-imagine. It was a wartime book, written between 1912 and 1918. It chose four public figures, none of them writers: a headmaster of a great public school, the nation's favourite wartime nurse-heroine, a powerful, ambitious priest who crossed from the Church of England to Rome, and one of Britain's most famous, and catastrophic, military leaders. All four – Dr Arnold, Florence Nightingale, Cardinal Manning, and General Gordon – had already had venerating biographical coverage (sources which Strachey plagiarized and distorted). All were ripe for debunking as figures whose formidable public activities could be reread as sublimations of private traumas and repression, and as representatives of a period considered, by its sceptical descendants, responsible for the carnage and shambles of the Great War.

Strachey set out his tactics in a Wildean preface which proposed to reject – and 'expose' – 'Victorian' heaviness, solemnity, and respect by light, ironic, irreverent methods. A 'little bucket' was to be lowered into the great ocean of the Victorian Age, which would 'bring up to the light of day some characteristic specimen, from those far depths, to be examined with a careful curiosity'. Scientific precision would lay bare what had been murky and hidden. Biography was to use unconventional angles of approach, attacking 'upon the flank, or the rear'. The military metaphors carried a knowing sexual nudge. This would be the Victorians unfrocked, with all their neuroses and secret appetites on show.

In fact, the essays were more emotional and sympathetic than the preface suggests. Strachey set Nightingale and Gordon, especially, as isolated, driven obsessives up against an incompetent English bureaucracy. He gave some touching pathos to defeated minor characters, like Cardinal Newman in the Manning essay and Arthur Hugh Clough in 'Florence Nightingale'. Certainly his tone was often sardonic, particularly with Dr Arnold, pillar of the single-sex public-school system, which Strachey's generation abominated for its philistinism, patriotic smugness, muscular Christianity, and unexamined sexual impact:

> Dr Arnold was never in any danger of losing his sense of moral evil. If the landscapes of Italy only served to remind him of it, how could he forget it among the boys at Rugby School? The daily sight of so many young creatures in the hands of the Evil One filled him with agitated grief.

But there were other tones in play, too. The family opposition Nightingale encountered is fictionalized as if in the voice of a fussing Victorian mother:

> It was very odd; what could be the matter with dear Flo? ... the curious thing was that she seemed to take no interest in husbands ... As if there was not plenty to do in any case, in the ordinary way, at home ...

The administrative blunders that sent Gordon to the Sudan are summed up with Johnsonian clarity:

> The whole history of his life, the whole bent of his character, seemed to disqualify him for the task for which he had been chosen. He was before all things a fighter, an enthusiast, a bold adventurer, and he was now to be entrusted with the conduct of an inglorious retreat.

The political agenda of *Eminent Victorians*, slyly expressed through tone and structure, was, like all biographical experiments, reacting against what came before. Now that we are not so familiar with Dean Stanley's awestruck 1844 Life of Dr Arnold, or with the post-Crimean War sanctification of Florence Nightingale as 'The Lady with the Lamp', it is harder to see why Strachey's book seemed so bold, funny, and shocking at the time. Later readers became irritated by the book's inaccuracies, dandyism, and (as the wise Iris Origo put it) its 'thinness' springing from 'condescension'. Strachey's later biographical experiments, Freudian readings of

Queen Victoria, paralysed by mourning (with an irreverent and much-imitated deathbed scene which ran back through her whole life in the flash of an eye), and of the sexually 'warped' Queen Elizabeth, now seem curiously old-fashioned. But *Eminent Victorians* was a flamboyantly pioneering work which provided a blueprint for all the modernist theorizing about biography.

Gosse's 1910 entry on 'Biography' in the *Encyclopaedia Brittanica* defined 'true' or 'pure' biography, 'the faithful portrait of a soul in its adventures through life', told without a moral agenda, as a 'very modern' conception. Writing in 1925 about his 17th-century hero Tallemant des Réaux, France's John Aubrey, author of some wicked 'miniature' lives (full of sentences like 'The Chevalier is a kind of lunatic, and moreover the greatest blasphemer in France'), Gosse praises him for being – like Strachey – 'never astonished and never indignant'. 'He wishes to set down the truth, and is not afraid of the facts.'

These 'modern' biographical ideals were echoed by a range of writers. Well before Gosse and Strachey, the French writer Marcel Schwob argued that short lives, preferably of obscure or eccentric characters, were the most suggestive. Quirks and curiosities and telling physical details – Cleopatra's nose, Alexander's drinking, Louis XIV's fistula – could speak more loudly than large historical events. Schwob set biography against history, arguing for the significance of the particular and the contingent over 'generalities and continuities'.

Harold Nicolson, diplomat, diarist, and husband of Vita Sackville-West, also argued for, and practised, short, artful, playful biography. Like Gosse, Nicolson set two kinds of biography against each other, the 'impure' (hagiographical, Victorian) and the 'pure' (truthful, well constructed, modern). This opposition of right/wrong, old/new, is a frequent and continuing tactic in biographical theorizing. But biography is always spilling out of such neat patterns. Nicolson foresaw a split between 'scientific' (sociological, psychoanalytical) and 'literary' (imaginative, crafted) biography, a stand-off that has never really taken place.

The French critic and biographer André Maurois claimed equal artistic status for biography with other arts in his 1928 Clark lectures, which deliberately borrowed the word 'Aspects' from E. M. Forster's *Aspects of the Novel*. Maurois' *Ariel*, his Life of Shelley, was intensely romantic. He thought biography should work, like poetry, through recurrent motifs (*Ariel* is full of water) and, like fiction, through an empathetic inwardness which would intuitively unlock the key to the subject's inner self. Emil Ludwig, author of psychological biographies of great German figures such as Goethe, Bismarck, and Wilhelm II, was also driven by an intuitive search for the essence of character. In America, Gamaliel Bradford, author of popular biographies and themed collections like *Saints and Sinners* (1931) and *Wives* (1925), coined 'psychography' for 'the condensed, essential, artistic presentation of character' and for the capturing, in a 'scientific spirit', of the complicated 'variance' of 'men's souls'.

There was an acute sense of that 'variance', of the gaps and contradictions within human beings. Between 1913 and 1927, Proust was publishing *À la recherche du temps perdu* (first translated into English between 1922 and 1932), his modern epic of the self in society, which examined in depth and at length the intermittencies and gaps in memory and identity. 'Relativity' was a new idea in physics. Concepts of what lay buried and hidden beneath the publicly functioning, or malfunctioning, self were making their way from Freudian psychoanalysis into literature.

Virginia Woolf's writings on biography – though shadowed by Leslie Stephen, Carlyle, Pater, Gosse, Strachey, Nicolson, and Proust – were original, and influential. Like other contemporary commentators, she had an evolutionary concept of it as a genre that needed to throw off the past and move towards some as yet unattained form. As with her writings on, and experiments in, 'modern fiction', she thought life-writing had to change in order to meet the new conditions of the 20th century. Having grown up with Leslie Stephen and the *Dictionary of National Biography*, she liked to set the 'new' biography against a caricatured version of Victorian Lives. But she was also very interested in Boswell, Carlyle, Hazlitt, and other creative figures in British biographical history, and her fascination with 'obscure' and 'eccentric' Lives had something in common with her father's policy of inclusion in the DNB.

Woolf was as interested in life-writing as in fiction. While her novels were trying out radically experimental ways of telling a life-story, she read a great deal of biography, wrote many vividly evocative sketches of other writers (dead ones in her essays, living ones – often ruthlessly satirized – in her diaries and letters), experimented with fictional biography, and wrote eloquent essays on the topic. In 'The New Biography' (1927), she argued for fearlessness, brevity, and vividness as 'modern', anti-Victorian biographical qualities. Facts needed to be manipulated, the true life was the inner life, there could be artistry, choice, and laughter. Character could be displayed in 'the tone of a voice, the turn of a head, some little phrase or anecdote picked up in passing'. But contemporary biography was not yet 'subtle and bold' enough to master the 'queer amalgamation' of 'granite and rainbow' – fact and vision, truth and art – that was needed.

In 'The Art of Biography' (1939), she was still arguing that the biographer – unlike the novelist – could never be 'free'. She was writing this while working on a commissioned life of her friend, the painter and art critic Roger Fry, which she found an intensely frustrating experience. She put the reasons for her difficulties into the essay. Any attempt at 'vision' in biography was hampered by 'facts'. But facts, she added, were unstable entities. 'What was thought a sin is now known, by the light of facts won for us by the psychologists, to be perhaps a misfortune; perhaps a curiosity ... The accent on sex has changed within living memory ... Many of the old chapter headings – life at college, marriage, career – are shown to be very arbitrary and artificial distinctions.' So the biographer's job was to be a pioneer, to 'go ahead of the rest of us, like the miner's canary' (the very choice of image suggests how facts change through time), 'testing the atmosphere, detecting falsity, unreality, and the presence of obsolete conventions'. In an age of 'a thousand cameras', the biographer's job was to 'admit contradictory versions of the same face'. The angle was changing, and so were our ideas of 'greatness' and 'smallness'.

At the heart of Woolf's critique of the genre is her sense that the inner life we all lead is never adequately reflected in biography. This is her most eloquent statement of the case:

> Here is the past and all its inhabitants miraculously sealed as in a magic tank; all we have to do is to look and to listen and to listen and to look and soon the little figures – for they are rather under life size – will begin to move and to speak, and as they move we shall arrange them in all sorts of patterns of which they were ignorant, for they thought when they were alive that they could go where they liked; and as they speak we shall read into their sayings all kinds of meanings which never struck them, for they believed when they were alive that they said straight off whatever came into their heads. But once you are in a biography all is different.

One answer to this intractable difficulty, an evasive and playful one, was to rewrite biography as comic, parodic fiction. *Flush* (1933) told the story of Elizabeth Barrett Browning through the eyes – and nose – of her spaniel. *Orlando* (1928), also subtitled 'A Biography', came equipped with full apparatus – acknowledgements, illustrations, index. It took its biographer, who appears as an unnamed, ungendered character, on a wild goose chase in pursuit of its subject. Orlando resists biographical conventions, changing from a man to a woman, living through three centuries, and refusing any determinants about identity, gender, and chronological progress. ('For she had a great variety of selves to call upon, far more than we have been able to find room for, since a biography is considered complete if it merely accounts for six or seven selves, whereas a person may well have as many thousand.')

By subverting biographical conventions through fictional parody, Woolf found a way of writing a teasing, private memoir of her friend and bisexual lover Vita Sackville-West which could be at once coded and revealing, erotic and censored. This new form of life-writing was also a feminist enterprise (though she did not call it that), which implied – as Woolf always argued – that women's lives required new forms of writing.

Could such playful, stylized fictional methods work as serious biographical tools? Other examples of the time read now, like *Orlando*, more as intriguing experiments in genre-busting than precedents for professional biography. Gertrude Stein invented a new language for telling the lives of obscure American women in *Three Lives* (1908), and turned autobiography and biography upside-down in the intimate, garrulous, boastful, gossipy *Autobiography of Alice B. Toklas* (1933). (Picasso's great, sturdy 1906 portrait of Stein is another example of how modernist experiments in art could create a powerful sense of character.) The art historian and Boswell editor Geoffrey Scott created, in *The Portrait of Zélide*, an elegantly dramatized life of the Dutch 18th-century writer Isabelle de Tuyl, who was connected to Voltaire, proposed to by Boswell, and loved by Benjamin Constant. A. J. A. Symons, Paterian aesthete and admirer of Wilde, wrote a biography of Frederick Rolfe, alias Baron Corvo, author of *Hadrian the Seventh*, failed priest, exile, unhappy homosexual, and venomous letter-writer, in the form of a pursuit of its elusive subject. *The Quest for Corvo* is part detective story, part spiritual journey, and part meditation on biography. Steeped in arcane learning, queer encounters, and fanciful symbolist prose, it is a very peculiar operation indeed, leaving the reader unconvinced that there was ever such a real person as Frederick Rolfe – or, possibly, his biographer.

11. Picasso's Stein: a powerful sense of character

Aestheticism – shaping, impressionism, artfulness – took biography in one direction. Most biographers of historical, political, or literary figures, however, were not primarily interested in formal experiments. Where aestheticians and historians, professional biographers and experimental life-writers did find themselves converging, from early in the 20th century, was through the powerful doctrines of Freudian psychoanalysis.

Sigmund Freud began publishing his findings on hysteria and psychology in the 1890s, and was being translated into English by Strachey's brother and sister-in-law, James and Alix Strachey, for the Hogarth Press, from the 1920s onwards. Freud praised *Elizabeth and Essex*, which showed, he thought, that Strachey was 'steeped in the spirit of psychoanalysis', enabling him to 'touch upon [Elizabeth]'s most hidden motives'. The practice of psychoanalysis as defined by Freud, and narrated in case-histories such as Dora, Little Hans, the Rat Man, or the Wolf Man, paralleled (and influenced) some of biography's processes: following clues, building up a pattern of behaviour, interpreting a whole personality through attending to significant details, deciding what was relevant, finding the hidden causes of adult behaviour in childhood. Freud compared the process to archaeological excavation, a metaphor that works for both analysis and biography. Yet Freud was extremely hostile to the genre.

> Anyone who writes a biography is committed to lies, concealments, hypocrisy, flattery and even to hiding his own lack of understanding, for biographical truth does not exist, and if it did we could not use it.

Adam Phillips quotes this letter of 1936 in an essay which argues that Freud saw 'the genre . . . as a kind of rival of his own discipline'. Freud's 'misgivings' about biography 'may also be his own displaced misgivings about psychoanalysis itself', Phillips suggests. If the 'true' self is hard to track back, even in analysis, how could biography hope to discover it? 'Freud hated biography because it represented the dangerous and misleading claims one person might make about knowing another person.' This, as Phillips notes wryly, created difficulties for Freud's own biographers, Ernest Jones and Peter Gay.

In the first example of 'psycho-biography', *Leonardo da Vinci and a Memory of Childhood* (1910), Freud interpreted Leonardo's life

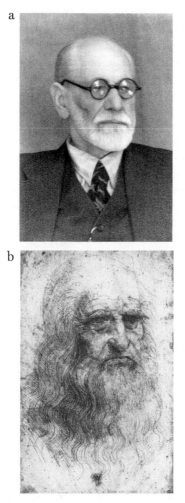

12. Sigmund Freud and Leonardo da Vinci. Psychoanalysis and the artist; a revolution in biography

and works as a story of neurosis, and homosexuality, produced by the repression of his childhood love of his mother. Part of that sexual repression was sublimated into 'a thirst for knowledge' – thus accounting both for Leonardo's strangeness, and his genius. This 'exhilaratingly speculative' analysis (based, notoriously, on the crucial mistranslation of a single word), shows a classic biographical tension 'between empirical observation and grand theory'. But, shaky or hypothetical though it may seem, it did throw down a forceful challenge to biographical censorship. Freud argued:

> If a biographical study really seeks to arrive at an understanding of the mental life of its hero, it must not – as most biographies do, out of discretion or prudery – keep silent about his sexual activity and sexual individuality.

Why should the exploration of a great man's pathology be felt to be distasteful? Because – he argued, weirdly – most biographers have an infantile fixation on their hero/subjects, and want to idealize them and turn them into their fathers. (Female biographers of female subjects do not exist for Freud.) Though their terms are different, Freud's claims for psychological investigation resemble the modernists' contemporaneous desire for a more daring, candid, and imaginative biographical practice.

Freud's influence on biography was immense. Even non-believers in psychoanalysis felt, post-Freud, a duty to deal with their subjects' sexuality, illnesses, dreams, and infancy. Anthony Storr notes:

> After psychoanalysis became established, biographers began to feel that, unless they had managed to uncover the emotional influences to which their subjects had been exposed during the earliest years of childhood, their portraits were incomplete.

Psycho-biography is out of fashion now, but vestigial traces of its language can be found (as in our everyday conversation), like a light scattering of snow, in contemporary biographies that are not remotely Freudian. So Claire Tomalin might speak of Jane Austen's 'childhood trauma' and 'depression', or Victoria Glendinning of Trollope's 'alienation'.

Psychoanalytical biography – sometimes fused with Marxist political analysis or sociological data – placed its subjects on the couch and fitted their behaviour into a pattern. Sartre's theory-driven literary biographies, indebted to both Freud and Marx, applied 'existential psychoanalysis' and sociological contextualizing to his subjects, in order to construct 'totalizing' accounts of the 'freedom and conditioning', which, for example, made Flaubert (*L'Idiot de la Famille*) both 'a neurotic and a great writer'. Sartre used his subjects to prove that 'a corpse is open to all comers'; or, to put it another way, 'that every man is perfectly knowable as long as one uses the appropriate methods and has available the necessary documents'. He applied a 'comprehensive synthesis which stopped only at death'. 'Total' biography could reveal a person's life 'as it was lived from within', and, at the same time, place the subjects 'as a product of their historical era, their class situation, and their childhood conditioning'. But Sartre's enormously detailed, controlling Lives of Genet and Flaubert, in which no illness is involuntary, no event contingent, no act inexplicable, leave many of his readers longing for 'inconclusiveness and disorder'. The narrator of Julian Barnes's *Flaubert's Parrot* comments:

> Look what happened to Flaubert: a century after his death Sartre, like some brawny, desperate lifeguard, spent ten years beating on his chest and blowing into his mouth; ten years trying to yank him back to consciousness, just so that he could sit him up on the sands and tell him exactly what he thought of him.

Erik Erikson's pioneering Freudian biography, *Young Man Luther* (1958), presented his subject in terms of 'a protracted identity crisis' arising from an Oedipal complex. Luther is 'beset with a syndrome of conflicts whose outline we have learned to recognize, and whose components to analyse'. So Luther's obsession with excrement is traced back 'to the beatings on his buttocks which he received as a child'. His 'identity crisis' began with a legendary fit he was supposed to have had in his twenties. Even if the fit did not actually happen, it could be accepted as 'half-history', provided it had a ring of truth and yielded 'a meaning consistent with psychological theory'.

From the 1920s to the 1960s (and even later), psycho-biography was a thriving genre. All sorts of writers, politicians, world leaders, composers, artists, scientists, and psychologists were put on the couch. Of course this aroused opposition. The American writer Bernard De Voto called psychoanalysis, in 1933, 'a preposterous instrument for the ascertaining of fact'. 'Psycho-analytical biography...does not tell us what did happen. It tells us instead what must have happened.' But Leon Edel maintained, in the 1950s, that the value of psychology, particularly for literary biography, was to show 'how the negatives were converted into positives', how the subject could overcome a 'wound' and turn it into art. His argument makes psycho-biography sound like medieval hagiography in its commitment to triumph over adversity. Richard Ellmann argued that psycho-biography could have its uses as long as 'it is the biographer manipulating psychological theory, not allowing psychological theory to manipulate him'. More recent commentators on psycho-biography tend to agree that its theory-driven, clinical approach had a distorting effect, and that the processes of psychoanalysis and biography have quite different aims.

Some of the most masterful literary lives of the mid-20th century – Leon Edel's *Life of Henry James* (1953–77), or George Painter's

Marcel Proust (1959) – now seem skewed by their psychoanalytical bias. Edel, reading James as formed by his father's subservience to his mother, rivalry with his brother, and a traumatic injury, analysed his fiction as often unconscious expressions of these experiences. So James's youthful observation of the dominance of women in his family is seen 'emerging' as a fictional 'vampire theme': 'Fear of women and worship of women: the love-theme plays itself out in striking fashion throughout Henry James's work. And usually love ... is a threat to life itself.' Arguing at one point from a list of names in one of James's notebooks, 'Ledward', 'Bedward', and 'Dedward', Edel proposed: 'To be led to the marriage bed was to be dead. Henry James accordingly chose the path of safety. He remained celibate.' Edel's James sometimes seems not to have known what he was doing as a writer, 'yielding to dictates deeper than those of the craft of authorship ... dictates of a psychological order'. 'The terms in which he talks of his father ... and of his brother ... tell a story the author never intended us to know, nor was fully aware of himself.' However rich and deep Edel's account of James's social, personal, and literary context, such moments in his biography seem over-schematic and infantilizing.

Painter's *Marcel Proust* was similarly theory-driven, unlocking the whole of Proust's life and work with the keys of 'mother' and 'illness'. Painter maintained that Proust 'invented nothing': his great literary achievement was not fiction but 'creative autobiography'. He drew on his own experience, synthesized and transformed it, to create 'a metaphorical representation of universal truths'. Working from internal evidence, Painter matched, with exhaustive and 'definitive' exactness, every piece of Proust's life to his work. (Strangely, he chose not to interview any of Proust's friends, many of whom were still alive while he was writing his biography.) The aim was 'to discover, beneath the mask of the artist's everyday, objective life, the secret life from which he extracted his work'.

Richard Ellmann's *Joyce*, another legendary mid-20th-century biography of literary 'genius', resisted such schematizing, and had fun with Joyce's mixed feelings about psychoanalysis. Joyce called Jung and Freud the Swiss Tweedledum and the Viennese Tweedledee, and had little time for Jung's analyses of *Ulysses*, or of his daughter Lucia, though he kept a dream diary and was deeply interested in the workings of the unconscious. Ellmann's method was not to psychoanalyse Joyce, though it happily used terms like 'Oedipal' and 'ambivalence'. It was to point everything in his life (and he tells us everything he can, in sympathetic, humorous, and eloquent detail) towards his work. His thesis is that of genius making shape and meaning out of the mundane and the messy. So there is a repeated note – as in more traditional, exemplary biography – of triumph and transcendence. At the end of *Ulysses*, 'the spirit is liberated from its bonds'. Such moments 'arise in quintessential purity from the mottled life of everyday'. Ellmann concludes his mighty book by insisting on the 'erratic and provisional' surface of Joyce's life and on what the 'splendid extravagance' of his work did with it, raising his life 'to dignity and high dedication'.

These three complex, intimate, supremely authoritative, much acclaimed biographies are now seen – as all biography comes to be seen – more as historical moments in the interpretations of those great writers' lives than as definitive monuments.

Modernist experiments and Freudian case-histories provided influential models for biography. Both fed into a thriving, rich, popular Anglo-American tradition of professional biography in the mid to late 20th century. Large-scale, realistic, thoroughly historicized Lives were energized by strong characterization and description, humour, candour, and intimacy. Many of them – like *Eminent Victorians* – took their subjects from the previous generation. It is an irony of biographical history that Lytton Strachey, the playful minimalist, should have been the subject of one of the first and biggest of these Lives. But it is apt, too.

Michael Holroyd's work (also on Augustus John and Shaw) followed Strachey's ethic of frankness, irony, impartiality, and vividness. His biography of Strachey echoed the sexual freedoms and political radicalism of the 1960s, and opened the door for a particularly strong phase of popular, respected British and Irish biography. Richard Holmes on Shelley and Coleridge; Claire Tomalin on Jane Austen and Pepys; Peter Ackroyd on Dickens; Victoria Glendinning on Rebecca West, Edith Sitwell, and Trollope; Hilary Spurling on Ivy Compton-Burnett and Matisse; Jenny Uglow on Gaskell and Hogarth; John Richardson on Picasso; Roy Foster on Yeats; Fiona McCarthy on William Morris and Eric Gill are a few outstanding examples.

At the same time, great numbers of solid, thoroughly researched professional and academic biographies of writers, artists, thinkers, politicians, scientists, and national leaders streamed out from (mainly) North American and European publishers. (Some magisterial specimens: Irvin Ehrenpreis's Swift (1962–83), Mark Schorer's Sinclair Lewis (1961), Walter Jackson Bates's Keats (1963), Justin Kaplan's Mark Twain (1966), Winifred Gérin's Charlotte Brontë (1967) and Gaskell (1976), Carlos Baker's Hemingway (1969), Ronald Paulson's Hogarth (1971, 1991–3), Arthur Mizener's Ford (1972), R. W. B. Lewis's Edith Wharton (1975), Matthew Bruccoli's Scott Fitzgerald (1981), Maynard Mack's Pope (1985).) No major – or, increasingly, minor – figure, in any field, now goes unbiographized. Many of these monuments to hard work and careful investigation are not self-consciously crafted, but set down, as fully and as accurately as possible, a chronological account of a significant life.

Though contemporary biography has not always been artful and selective, it does pay a debt to modernist discussions and practice of the genre, in its belief in truth-telling, humour, and realism, its emphasis on childhood and sexuality, its explorations of inner lives as much as public achievements, and its reluctance (with a few notorious exceptions) to moralize, take sides, or cast blame. Yet biography can still involve acts of piety. Though it wants to be truthful and frank, it can still find itself in thrall to censoring pressures, and may still have to grapple with stories that can only be partially told, disappearing evidence, reluctant or forbidding subjects. The same challenges and contradictions recur.

Chapter 6
Against Biography

The literary case against biography partly has its roots in aestheticism, in the idea of the separateness and purity – or amorality – of the work of art. The examples of Flaubert and the French symbolist poets fuelled an argument for art as an inviolable entity, set apart from the life, not to be degraded by biographical interpretation. For Baudelaire, for example, 'poetry is both distinguished from and elevated above the world in which it exists'. The artist-as-person – what Yeats famously called 'the bundle of accident and incoherence that sits down to breakfast' – was meant to be quite distinct from the artist in the work. 'The more perfect the artist, the more completely separate in him will be the man who suffers and the mind which creates.' T. S. Eliot's high claim for artistic separateness was shared by James, Yeats, Ford, and other modernist writers dedicated to constructing their own original, free-standing, authoritative aesthetic systems, masks, and patterns – however interested they might also be in biographies of other writers. Joyce, who invented the 'biografiend' or 'beogrefright' in *Finnegans Wake*, made the ultimate claim for artistic impersonality and invisibility in *A Portrait of the Artist*: 'The artist, like the God of creation, remains within or behind or beyond or above his handiwork, invisible, refined out of existence, indifferent, paring his fingernails.' Such modernist manifestos had a lasting effect on the Anglo-American academic school of 'new criticism', which rejected biography as a 'fallacious quest for the origins of works: fallacious, because anything relevant to an autonomous work was by definition contained within it'. Modernism's hostility to biography also influenced the French *nouveau roman*, whose authors, such as Alain Robbe-Grillet, argued for 'a conception of authorship defined purely in terms of formal awareness', and late 20th-century critical theories (notably voiced by Roland Barthes) of 'the death of the author'.

That theoretical separation of text and life created a long stand-off between biography viewed as a popular, impure, conservative, and unexamined product for consumption by the general reader, and the academic study of literature and history. From the mid to late 20th century, it was often noted (regretfully, or happily) that biography 'has remained notably untheorised', that it has had 'a lack of legitimacy in the worlds of contemporary critical theory [and] social historiography', and has 'seemed insufficiently substantial or scientific to merit study or teaching'. It is only recently that biography has become a regular subject for books and essays, and an established academic discipline. For example, the University of Hawaii has had a Center for Biographical Research since 1978; courses and departments of Life-Writing have been set up in several British universities; there is a Biography Institute at the Australian National University in Canberra, a Center for Biography at City University in New York, and an Institute in Vienna dedicated to the 'systematic' study of the History and Theory of Biography.

Meanwhile, biographies for the general reader, especially of non-literary figures, have largely ignored these critical arguments and academic debates. Popular biography, ranging from downmarket tabloid-style packages on media figures to solidly researched, lavishly illustrated lives of politicians or historical leaders, is a thriving industry (though every so often there will be predictions of doom from the publishing industry about 'the death of biography', as there used to be about 'the death of the novel'). But with the popularity and ubiquity of biography goes a good deal of fear and loathing. Hostility to biography can take the form not of an aesthetic critique, but of the same kind of ethical objections to its intrusiveness which might have been made against Edmund Curll, or by Tennyson or Henry James. This usually arises when there is a conflict between the 'keepers of the flame' and the 'publishing scoundrels'. The case against biography was forcefully made by the American writer Janet Malcolm in the 1990s, when she involved herself in the painful battle between Sylvia Plath's biographers and Ted Hughes, whose lifelong efforts to defend his and his children's privacy, to control the publication of Plath's archive, and to monitor what was published of Plath's or about Plath, led to much vilification from Plath's advocates:

Biography is the medium through which the remaining secrets of the famous dead are taken from them and dumped out in full view of the world. The biographer at work, indeed, is like the professional burglar, breaking into a house, rifling through certain drawers that he has good reason to think contain the jewelry and money, and triumphantly bearing his loot away. The voyeurism and busybodyism that impel writers and readers of biography alike are obscured by an apparatus of scholarship designed to give the enterprise an appearance of banklike blandness and solidity. The biographer is portrayed almost as a kind of benefactor. He is seen as sacrificing years of his life to his task, tirelessly sitting in archives and libraries and patiently conducting interviews with witnesses. There is no length he will not go to, and the more his book reflects his industry the more the reader believes that he is having an elevating literary experience, rather than listening to backstairs gossip and reading other people's mail. The transgressive nature of biography is rarely acknowledged, but it is the only explanation for biography's status as a popular genre. The reader's amazing tolerance (which he would extend to no novel written half as badly as most biographies) makes sense only when seen as a kind of collusion between him and the biographer in an excitingly forbidden undertaking: tiptoeing down the corridor together, to stand in front of the bedroom door and try to peep through the keyhole.

Malcolm's rhetoric (of ransacking, burglary, voyeurism, violation) echoes 19th-century expressions of horror at the exposure of private lives. But biography has much more licence now, and often gets away with murder. Newspaper articles called 'Biography as a Blood Sport', or describing 'The Business of Biography' as 'digging up the traumatic, the indefensible, and the shameful and getting it all into print', regularly remind us of the genre's ancient, discreditable links to scandal and slander.

It is possible to talk about biography almost entirely in terms of exposure, titillation, and shock, as in a 1990s essay by Justin Kaplan, who maintains that 'by current standards, biographies without voyeuristic, erotic thrills are like ballpark hot dogs without mustard'. He cites several examples of sensational or vindictive Lives, like Kitty Kelley's book on Nancy Reagan, which he describes as essentially a 'drive-by shooting', and of outraged attacks on biography from its victims. Germaine Greer, for instance, threatened with an unwelcomed Life, called biography a form of 'rape . . . an unpardonable crime against selfhood', and described biographers of living writers as 'the intellectual equivalents of flesh-eating bacterium'. Natasha Spender bitterly protested at the 'prurient interest' and 'fundamental errors' of an unauthorized biography of her husband Stephen Spender, at the 'invasive techniques' of some biographers and the 'serious, incalculable injury' they can cause.

Efforts by living subjects or their relatives and executors to control the biographer can backfire. Salinger's court case against Ian Hamilton led to the withdrawal of the biography Hamilton wanted to publish, but then to a book which described in revealing detail Salinger's obstruction of the process. Nadine Gordimer's withdrawal of authorization from a biographer she had initially approved and encouraged, because of his violation of their agreement to address any objections she posed, and his refusal to remove passages of which she did not approve, exposed her to just the kind of gossipy publicity she had wanted to avoid. Ronald

13. **Popular biography as media product: intrusion and sensation**

Against Biography

Suresh Roberts's highly proprietorial, judgemental, anecdotal narrative, brimming with his own opinions on personal and political matters, as well as with close readings of her work and a great deal of interesting source material, was refused by Gordimer's publishers in New York and London, who had originally agreed to publish it, on the grounds that it was no longer 'authorized'. So Roberts placed it with a South African press (which exported copies), prominently incorporated into the book early expressions of enthusiasm for him by Gordimer and her publishers, and went public, in numerous interviews, with details of all the material she had not wanted him to include, and sarcastic remarks about the paradoxical contrast between Gordimer's own resistance to the repressive era of apartheid and her 'censoring' of his work: 'She is supposed to represent freedom of speech but she wanted complete control.' Gordimer withdrew into dignified silence on the matter, hoping, no doubt, that her work would outlast his.

When poets and novelists object to biography, it is often not so much for ethical or protectionist reasons as because biography seems to them a reductionist simplification, a grotesque travesty of what they do, and an interference with a writer's main ambition – which is to be judged by, and remembered for, their writing. Sometimes they make sure to get in first. Doris Lessing, in the first volume of her autobiography in *Under My Skin* (1994), said, with typical sharpness: 'You cannot sit down to write about yourself without rhetorical questions of the most tedious kind demanding attention.' One is 'Why an autobiography at all?' The answer was: 'Self-defence; biographies are being written.' When writers put imaginary biographers into their work, they are usually portrayed as monsters of cynicism, opportunism, tactlessness, or tin-eared stupidity. So Jake Bolokowsky in Larkin's 'Posterity' is a bored, crude young American using his subject, Philip Larkin ('One of those old-type *natural* fouled-up guys') as a necessary step to academic advancement, and Carol Ann Duffy's vain, shallow, and self-seeking biographer ruthlessly appropriates his 'Main Man': 'In all of your mirrors, my face;/with its smallish, quizzical eyes,/its cheekbones, its sexy jaw,/its talentless, dustjacket smile.'

Fictional biographers are usually characterized as parasites, obsessives, or stalkers. They turn up in contemporary novels such as (among many others) Penelope Lively's *According to Mark*, Alison Lurie's *The Truth about Lorin Jones*, A. S. Byatt's *Possession* and *The Biographer's Tale*, Kingsley Amis's *The Biographer's Moustache*, Bernard Malamud's *Dubin's Lives*, William Golding's *The Paper Men*, and Philip Roth's *Exit Ghost*. In *Exit Ghost* (2007), for example, the ageing novelist Nathan Zuckerman tries to protect the reputation of the long-dead hero and mentor of his youth, the reclusive writer E. I. Lonoff, from the predatory assault of a 'rampaging would-be biographer'. Both Zuckerman and the woman who cherishes Lonoff's memory express their dread of biography as a form of reductivism and exposure, the trespassing of an 'inferior' talent onto a major life, motivated by the desire 'to expose the writer to censure'. Zuckerman, asking himself if he will be the biographer's next target, after Lonoff, exclaims to himself: 'An astonishing thing it is, too, that one's prowess and achievement, such as they have been, should find their consummation in the retribution of biographical inquisition.'

When it is not being anathematized, biography in fiction is the subject of sceptical novelistic enquiry, most famously here in a much-quoted image from Julian Barnes's *Flaubert's Parrot*:

> You can define a net in one of two ways, depending on your point of view. Normally, you would say that it is a meshed instrument designed to catch fish. But you could, with no great injury to logic, reverse the image and define a net as a jocular lexicographer once did: he called it a collection of holes tied together with string.
>
> You can do the same with a biography. The trawling net fills, then the biographer hauls it in, sorts, throws back, stores, fillets and sells. Yet consider what he doesn't catch: there is always far more of that.

The biography stands, fat and worthy-burgherish on the shelf, boastful and sedate: a shilling life will give you all the facts, a ten pound one all the hypotheses as well. But think of everything that got away, that fled with the last death bed exhalation of the biographee.

To be 'against' biography, for moral or aesthetic, personal or professional reasons, is almost always to be involved in an argument about property, ownership, and control. Such arguments are liable to be fraught and painful, full of rivalry and jealousy, competitiveness and mistrust. Biography is not neutral ground: it arouses strong and passionate feelings. There is despair, anger, even hopelessness, in Ted Hughes's cry: 'I hope each of us owns the facts of his or her own life.'

Chapter 7
Public Roles

For the biographer, who himself represents the social world, the social self is the real self; the self only comes to exist when juxtaposed with other people. The solitary self is a pressure upon the social self, or a repercussion of it, but it has no independent life.

A great man ... finds himself modelled by the function he has to perform; unconsciously he aims at making his life a work of art ... and so he acquires ... that statuesque quality that makes him a fine model for the artist.

Defensive and protective practices comprise the techniques employed to safeguard the impression fostered by an individual during his presence before others ... The expressive coherence that is required in performances points out a crucial discrepancy between our all-too-human selves and our socialized selves. As human beings we are presumably creatures of variable impulse with mood and energies that change from one moment to the next. As characters put on for an audience, however, we must not be subject to ups and downs.

These observations by Richard Ellmann, André Maurois, and Erving Goffman all describe individual lives as constructed performances played out in a public arena, shaped by choices and functions, and dependent upon reception and recognition. The description does not only apply to 'great men': we all construct a 'presentation of the self'. The social anthropologist Erving

Goffman also talks about 'impression management' and 'the whole machinery of self-production'. Sometimes, as he observes, the performance breaks down, or is exposed as a cynical strategy, or is constructed at too great a cost. He cites Sartre's witty example of 'the attentive pupil who wishes to *be* attentive, his eyes riveted on the teacher, his ears open wide', who 'so exhausts himself in playing the attentive role that he ends up by no longer hearing anything'.

What is biography's relation to the performative aspect of identity, the individual's public role? The more public the subject of a biography, the more urgent the question becomes. The obvious answer – the one Plutarch gave, and commentators like Bacon and Dryden approved of – is that biography's job is to get behind the public performance and show us the real person at home in his 'undress'. But the quotations above suggest that a real self may be very hard to disentangle from a performed, public, social self. Richard Ellmann's insistence on biography as a record of the 'social self' implies that the biographer can have nothing to say about any other kind of self.

When Henry James met Robert Browning for the first time, in 1877, he was amazed at his unpoetic, vulgar, chattering, public self. He decided, half joking, that there must be '2 Brownings – an esoteric and an exoteric. The former never peeps out in society, and the latter hasn't a ray of suggestion of *Men & Women*.' This thought inspired, later, a story called 'The Private Life', where the narrator, baffled by the public performance of a much-admired writer, realizes that there are *two* of him: 'One goes out, the other stays at home. One is the genius, the other's the bourgeois.'

Literary biographers usually try not to split the performing, public, everyday self off from the private writing self, but to work out the connection between them. That is really the whole point of literary biography, though it can be done well or badly. For biographers of philosophers, the relation between the two performances, the life and the work, is a more contested area. It is often maintained that there can be only two schools of thought about this, as follows: 'The first contends that biography holds the secret to understanding the work of a philosopher, the second that the understanding of a philosopher's life is irrelevant to an understanding of his [sic] work.' It could be argued that a philosopher's writing may have as little to do with his, or her, private life as a set of mathematical propositions or a chemical formula might have to do with the mathematician's divorce or the chemist's breakfast. But it seems more plausible to argue for a middle ground. It could be the case that for certain kinds of philosophers – Augustine, Wittgenstein, Socrates – the life *is* the work, or the life has a bearing, if an oppositional one, to the work. So it could be said of Socrates (who wrote nothing) that 'his life is his work and his work is his life'. Philosophical commentators on Wittgenstein's work on language and ethics, the *Tractatus*, frequently point to the same kind of connection: 'No one who reads, or tries to read the *Tractatus*, can help wondering what kind of person its author was.... The more we know of him as a person, the more interesting become the connections, and disconnections, to his philosophical work.' 'He offered himself up in his philosophizing.' 'It would be hard to invent a life whose inner travails and self imposed adversities might better illustrate the perplexities that arise from Wittgenstein's philosophy of life.' Statements of Wittgenstein's such as 'If you are unwilling to know what you are, your writing is a form of deceit', or 'You cannot write anything about yourself that is more truthful than you yourself are', are likely to make his commentators want to connect a personal appraisal and a philosophical one. Ray Monk's biography of Wittgenstein shows that he 'neither wanted to, nor thought he could, separate the task of becoming the sort of human being he wanted to be from the task of being the sort of philosopher he wanted to be'.

Philosophy and biography are connected, too, because questions that occupy some philosophers (Descartes, or Heidegger) about the reality of the self and how we can make sense of ourselves, are questions with which biography is also concerned. Biography could be said to resemble philosophy in its aim. As Wittgenstein describes it, and as Ray Monk argues, that aim is to arrive at 'the kind of understanding that consists in seeing connections'. Biographical anxieties about how a narrative construction can represent a 'real' life or self may parallel, or come close to, philosophical arguments about how human actions can be presented and understood. Philosophy, indeed, can reassure biographers on this point. If, in the philosopher Alasdair MacIntyre's formulation, 'human actions' are 'enacted narratives', if 'we all live out narratives in our lives and . . . understand our lives in terms of the narratives that we live out', then 'the form of narrative is appropriate for understanding the actions of others'. It may be that the validity of such narratives will depend, as in philosophy, on how the story is constructed, 'with what degree of particularity'. But, whatever the specific qualities of the storyteller, biographers need not fear (as at least some philosophers argue) that 'to give a narrative account of a human life is necessarily to falsify it'.

Where a life is all action and narrative, rather than words or ideas, different kinds of challenges are presented to the biographer. What does biography do with subjects whose achievements consist entirely of public activities (politicians, bankers, doctors), whose life's work may be non-verbal (composers, painters, mathematicians, athletes), or who express themselves through performing others' words or music (actors, singers, pianists)? How does biography tell the story of such public roles, or penetrate to the secret selves of figures who are – as Henry James said of Theodore Roosevelt – 'pure act'?

Biographies of leaders or activists must set the central performance of their subjects in the context of the political conditions that produce them, the society in and on which they operate, their race, class, nationality, and gender, and the many other figures who surround them. Biographers have to be aware of changing views – including their own view – of their subject's profession. The life, say, of a 19th-century Christian missionary in Africa is likely to be approached differently now than it would have been a hundred and fifty years ago. Biographies of sports personalities, rock stars, or film actors have to deal not only with an individual personality and life-story, but also with the army of talent-spotters, promoters, managers, agents, producers, backers, publicists, photographers, directors, writers, and audiences who surround and often create the central performance. No Life of Elvis could afford to ignore Colonel Tom Parker; no group biography of the Beatles would miss out Brian Epstein. Any life that is acted out through a profession, whether that of a judge or a gardener, a conductor or a cook, requires the biographer to grasp the network of forces and the social assumptions which surround that profession at that time and in that place, to look at how attitudes to the subject, and their profession, may have shifted through time, and to work out the relationship between public performance and identity.

And any public life will have its secrets, its peculiarities, and its contradictions, which it is the biographer's job first to discover and then to understand. There is no more humorous or touching commentary on this than W. H. Auden's 1930s sonnet, 'Who's Who', on the unaccountable private life of a heroic public man:

A shilling life will give you all the facts:
How Father beat him, how he ran away,
What were the struggles of his youth, what acts
Made him the greatest figure of his day:
Of how he fought, fished, hunted, worked all night,
Though giddy, climbed new mountains; named a sea:
Some of the last researchers even write
Love made him weep his pints like you and me.

With all his honours on, he sighed for one
Who, say astonished critics, lived at home;
Did little jobs about the house with skill
And nothing else; could whistle; would sit still
Or potter round the garden; answered some
Of his long marvellous letters but kept none.

The poem is at once a love-story, a satire on the limits of biography, and a meditation on life's choices – where the second figure stands as the first figure's alternative life, his 'road not taken'. And it suggests that some other kind of life-writing – quite different from the standard, cliché'd 'shilling life' – is needed for the second figure, the obscure beloved, living quietly in the everyday, not caring about fame or immortality.

One mighty example of the challenge to the biographer of a public life is the American financier and art collector J. P. Morgan, 'the most powerful banker in the world', whose ambitions, force, and control invite comparisons with his favourite childhood hero, Napoleon. Jean Strouse, Morgan's biographer, who started her work on him about seventy years after his death, had to master not only the enormous (and largely untapped) archive in the Pierpont Morgan Library, but also, for this quintessentially American story, big business, banking, the stock market, the press and politics at the end of the 19th century, the history of the American railroads, the steel industry, international shipping, museums, collecting, house decoration, and Gilded Age society. Meanwhile she was dealing with a character notorious for his defensiveness and oddness, 'brusque, publicity shy, neither introspective nor articulate', magnetic, forceful, depressive, hypochondriacal, conservative, sexually susceptible and unfaithful, greedy, acquisitive, and philanthropic. Sometimes it must have been hard to get beyond the notorious nose.

And there was a further problem. Attitudes to Morgan had been largely fixed for a century: he was 'exalted by the right as a hero of economic progress and vilified by the left as an icon of capitalist greed'. As her years of work went on, Strouse found she was too wedded to her preconception of a 'cynical tycoon'. The evidence she was unearthing was altering the picture. Against the grain of her own assumptions, she painstakingly recast her narrative to give a more truthful and complex picture.

Such revisionary work, and rethinking of myths, is likely to form part of any serious Life of a public figure. Secular hagiography does continue to be written. Idealized, exemplary Lives often serve, still, as elegies for representatives of victimized minorities, revolutionary leaders, political prisoners, or spokespersons for the oppressed. There is a huge political and cultural investment for certain groups in maintaining an inviolable biographical image of figures such as Gandhi, Steve Biko, Mother Theresa, Martin Luther King, Rosa Luxembourg, Che Guevara, or, above all, Nelson Mandela. A recent analysis by Elleke Boehmer of the 'heroic symbolization' of Mandela as 'secular saint and architect of democracy', a global and national 'icon' who has been 'over-represented to the point of being rendered banal, excavated for meaning till all sense of the human being behind the public face disappears', argues that it is impossible for biographers in South Africa, or elsewhere, to write about him except in terms of his 'national symbolic significance'. Biographical representation is always entangled here with oral testimony, journalism, biopics, documentary film, and 'iconic' photographs, like emblematic images of Che Guevara in his beret (on every Western Marxist student's wall or T-shirt in the 1960s), or lying like Mantegna's dead Christ, bullet-ridden in the hospital in Bolivia. Sanctification, in most cases, then produces backlash, which veers to the other extreme of vilification. So Mother Theresa's self-serving, right-wing politics, Luther King's sexual exploits, or Guevara's thuggish killings in the Havana jails and his treatment of homosexuals are aired in myth-debunkings which, in turn, serve their own political and cultural purpose.

The politics of biography come sharply into focus when the subject stands for, or inspires, a debate about national myths and character, as with the emphasis on 'national biography' in the 19th century. Churchill, Thatcher, De Gaulle come to mind; so, especially, does Horatio Nelson, England's greatest naval hero. The *New DNB* entry on Nelson describes his afterlife as an 'apotheosis', beginning with paintings of him 'at the moment he was struck

14. **Che Guevara: The making and unmaking of a legend**

down in compositions closely modelled on the deposition of Christ
from the cross'. A 2004 biography of Nelson by John Sugden, a
naval historian, tackles at length the challenge of a much-
mythologized public life. Sugden takes over 900 pages to get
Nelson halfway through his career. His story starts with Nelson's
death in 1805, and the erecting of more than 'thirty monuments to
his memory'. 'Biographies of Nelson are also monuments', he notes,
'and equally reflect shifting opinion'. The early two-volume life by
James Clarke and John McArthur, published in 1809, relied
heavily on what Sugden calls Nelson's 'self-congratulatory
fragment' of autobiography, which represented his own life as an
exemplary story of perseverance, heroic deeds, and public duty.
Nelson's long and scandalous relationship with Lady Emma
Hamilton was well known, so the authors could not plead
ignorance, but 'merely declared the subject off limits', and
concentrated instead on his 'splendid public character'. Southey's
heroic Life of 1813 'cemented the admiral's status as the authentic
British hero'. (Though Southey, as he said himself, was no naval
expert: 'I walk among sea terms as a cat goes in a china pantry, in
bodily fear of doing mischief, & betraying myself.') A thorough,
candid Life of 1849 by Thomas Pettigrew was 'hissed out of print'
because it proved that Nelson's child was the product of his
adultery. At the end of the 19th century, biographies of Nelson
presented him as 'the ultimate exemplar of naval achievement'. The
DNB notes that the Navy League was promoting 'the cult of
Trafalgar day' in the years before the First World War, with Nelson
as 'a symbol of imperial Britain and its overarching sea-power, and
a talisman against anxiety... Nelson the man... had largely been
forgotten in Nelson the hero.' His ardour, naivety, arrogance,
energy, lack of diplomatic skills, emotional susceptibility, and
egotism had all been smoothed away into a monument.

During the Second World War, Nelson's heroic image came in
useful again. Sugden notes that 'a remarkably wooden Laurence
Olivier... portrayed the admiral in a British film designed to win
American hearts to a crusade against the European dictators.'

A well-researched 1946 biography by Carola Oman and the editing of Nelson's letters in 1958 deepened the picture. But in the 1960s, Sugden maintains, naval history became unfashionable, and Nelson's patriotic virtues seemed 'outmoded'. Attention focused increasingly on his sexual rather than his naval conquests, culminating in a 'bravely irreverent' but at times 'vindictive'

15. Nelson: The national hero and his memorabilia

biography by Terry Coleman in 2001. Sugden promises his readers to set aside 'idolatry' and 'denigration' in favour of 'dispassionate judgment'. Yet, though he brings out Nelson's mixed qualities, his rhetoric is not quite free of heroic cadences: 'Nelson always identified his cause with that of the nation. Whether acting rightly or wrongly, he represented his struggle as one for the good of the realm. His honour was his country's honour, and his triumphs the country's triumphs.' Old biographical traditions die hard.

Nelson was loved and venerated; tyrants and mass murderers raise different problems for biographers. A tendency towards sycophancy in some political biographers, which has led Michael Holroyd to call them 'history's butlers', is not the problem if the subject is Hitler, Stalin, Nero, Idi Amin, Pol Pot, or Robert Mugabe. Baleful, destructive public lives require biographical steadiness and clarity, especially when the myth has outgrown reality, or when, like Napoleon or Alexander the Great, the subjects have been romanticized as much as vilified.

Psychoanalytical treatments of notorious public figures – Hitler as the product of childhood trauma – have had a lasting currency. Intriguing examples are Rebecca West's 1947 account of the Irish Nazi propagandist William Joyce, 'Lord Haw Haw', as a study of an inferiority complex, or Nicholas Mosley's painful memoir of his father Oswald Mosley, which is all about control: 'He felt he could order the world as he ordered words.' Less theory-driven accounts of appalling public figures, like Alan Bullock's double biography of Hitler and Stalin, concentrate on facts and context, though even this thoughtful approach can allow itself to express outrage:

> The indelible impression left by [*Mein Kampf's*] seven hundred pages is the vulgarity of Hitler's mind, cunning and brutal...intolerant and devoid of human feeling...But no less striking is the consistency and systematic character of his views, however crude. The struggle for existence is a law of Nature; hardness is the supreme virtue...power is the prerogative of a racial

elite; the masses are capable only of carrying out orders ... force is the only means by which anything lasting is accomplished ... Stalin would have found little to disagree with. Together they represent the twentieth century's most formidable examples of those '*simplificateurs terribles*' whom the nineteenth-century historian, Jakob Burckhardt, foresaw as characteristic of the century to follow.

This measured tone contrasts sharply with a more recent, more populist version of Stalin. Simon Sebag Montefiore had the 21st-century advantage of gaining access to hitherto inaccessible archives and sources in Russia. His *Stalin: The Court of the Red Tzar* (2004) and *Young Stalin* (2007) pursued the staggering facts of Stalin's career with the boisterous drive of an adventure story or a thriller, avoiding psychoanalytical interpretations or historical moralizings, but every so often pausing to remind us that this rollicking yarn is the story of a psychopathic mass murderer. This is the roller-coaster version of tragic world history, biography not as sombre meditation but as action and event.

A regime such as Stalin's obliterated millions of lives, produced millions of unwritten biographies. Such phases in history, when so much human story is wiped out, and so much can only be reconstructed through oral testimony, silent photographs, or horrified guesswork, at once destabilize and intensify the value of life-writing. We want to find out everything we can about the life of, say, Anne Frank; at the same time, we are aware of the vast numbers of obliterated life-stories whose particularities we will never know.

Exceptional lives with strong public resonance emerging from such wastelands of history are likely to be especially contested. One of the most potent lives to have survived Stalinism was that of the composer Shostakovich, a tremendously complex subject for biography. Shostakovich's gigantically productive musical life (1906–75) spanned the Russian Revolution, the war, Stalin's murderous and repressive regime, with its mass purges and its silencing of artists, the straitjacket of 'socialist realism', Communism, the Cold War, and the cultural thaw. He received every kind of accolade and attack, from early fame to party threats, from criticisms of his 'compromised' musical manifestos to posthumous, post-Soviet-era revisionist claims for his irony and concealed subversiveness. Shostakovich's understandable refusal to speak out about his work except in 'sweeping platitudes' or enforced apologias, his holding back in secret of some works for many years, his complex, coded musical use of self-references and allusions, and the official titles often attached to his pieces, all make for biographical bafflement.

The huge changes in Russia during and after his lifetime produced dramatic shifts of attitudes towards him. Soviet obituaries and early biographies celebrated his assertion of 'the ideals of Soviet humanism and internationalism'. The reputation was startlingly altered by the publication in 1979 of the *Testimony* of Solomon Volkov, his devoted acolyte in later years, who claimed to be transcribing Shostakovich's private conversation – bitter, ironical, self-reproachful, subversive – and who described him as a '*yurodivy*', a 'holy fool'. But Volkov's reliability has been much questioned. As large numbers of first-hand descriptions and letters began to surface, and as Shostakovich's reputation as a great composer spread, biographers had to step clear of 'speculation and ideological tendentiousness'. Laurel Fay's meticulous, careful Life of 2000 picked its way through startlingly different versions of her subject. She comments:

> Writing about Shostakovich remains laced with political and moral subtexts. At its most extreme, it simply replaces one orthodoxy with another . . . The true-believing Communist citizen-composer is inverted into an equally unconvincing caricature of a lifelong closet dissident. . . . There is pressing need to sort . . . the man from the myths.

The difficulty that always arises in trying to read music directly back into the life of the composer is compounded by the long battle

16. The self-concealing composer: the life in the work

for survival which cloaked Shostakovich's motives and intentions. His best-known quartet, for example, the Eighth (written in 1960), an intensely and powerfully emotional piece, was written after a visit to Dresden and is said by some commentators to be a 'literal evocation of the Dresden bombings'. It was also, however, written soon after he had suffered what Laurel Fay calls an 'emotional breakdown' in response to being forced to become a member of the Communist Party, a recruitment which he had previously resisted. Volkov quoted him as saying that the quartet, though 'assigned to the department of "exposing fascism"', was 'autobiographical'. The quartet's allusions to earlier works, and his use of a repeated motif based on the initials of his own name, made this clear to anyone who was not 'blind'. A letter of 1960 corroborates Volkov: 'I've written this ideologically flawed quartet which nobody will be interested in ... "Dedicated to the memory of the composer of this quartet", could be written on the title page.' In 2002, Shostakovich's daughter Galina remembered her father saying: 'I've just written a composition which I've dedicated to my own memory.' But after the quartet's success he was persuaded to change the dedication 'to the victims of fascism'. This dedication may have been forced upon him, but (as his son, Maxim Shostakovich, argued) it could, indeed, be read autobiographically. 'If you take "fascism" to mean "totalitarianism" the ambivalence disappears. Shostakovich was one of countless victims of a monstrous totalitarian regime.' Laurel Fay steps through these ambiguities by describing the quartet's powerful effect on its first listeners, who, though 'misdirected in their understanding of the ... substance of the quartet ... were stunned by its tragic depth'. They recognized that it was autobiographical 'in its essence', even if the quartet's many quotations from his own earlier scores and the insistent use of his 'motto' were thought to refer to his 'struggle against the dark forces of reaction'.

Those forces pressed especially hard on Shostakovich in the period from 1936 to 1937. After the popular success of his opera, *Lady Macbeth of the Mtsensk District*, he was threateningly denounced in a notorious article in *Pravda*, headed 'Muddle instead of Music'. Shostakovich was said to have contemplated suicide. He was writing his Fourth Symphony, with its two long, dark outer movements, its funeral march, and its slow fading away into *pianissimo* and silence. The symphony was finished in 1936, but was withdrawn from public performance, either because of external pressure, or his fear of reprisals. It was kept in a drawer for twenty-five years, and not performed until 1961. Instead, in 1937, he produced his Fifth Symphony, a more traditional work, with a hammering triumphal ending, greeted with huge public acclaim. It was given the subtitle 'A Soviet Artist's Practical Creative Reply to Just Criticism', a subtitle probably provided by a journalist, though Shostakovich gave it his tacit assent, perhaps 'as a subterfuge to assist in his rehabilitation'. After the Fifth Symphony's success, he said to the conductor Boris Khaikin (who did not then know about the Fourth Symphony): 'I finished the symphony *fortissimo* and in the major. Everyone is saying that it's an optimistic and life-affirming symphony. I wonder, what would they be saying if I had finished it *pianissimo* and in the minor?' In the 1970s, he told Volkov:

> I think that it is clear to everyone what happens in the Fifth. The rejoicing is forced, created under a threat...It's as if someone were beating you with a stick and saying, 'Your business is rejoicing, your business is rejoicing' and you rise, shakily, and go marching off muttering, 'Our business is rejoicing, our business is rejoicing.' What kind of apotheosis is that?

Shostakovich's life provides a major challenge for biographers, in matters such as reading the life from the work, trusting witnesses, understanding the historical context, deciding what to believe, trying to track the hidden agenda of a public life and – above all – explaining genius.

Other kinds of biographical challenges are presented by lives lived entirely through performance, celebrity lives that seem to make themselves completely available in the public domain.

Commentary on such figures – especially if they are women – is profuse and relentless, much of it quick, ephemeral, invented, and intrusive. The scandals and tragedies of their lives seem part of their performances, produced by the conditions of fame. Their visual images fuel gigantic media sales, in some cases long after their deaths. Yet – or therefore – they may remain biographically puzzling or impenetrable, swallowed up by their own myth. The kind of celebrities who become sufficiently famous to be known by a single name – Garbo, Callas, Diana, Elvis, Piaf, Madonna, Dylan – require their biographers to sort out 'iconic' image from reality, myth from fact, surface from depth. And there is always a risk that there may be no depth after all, only appearance and performance.

The most alluring and insoluble of all such modern biographical subjects is, probably, still, 'Marilyn'. There are huge numbers of biographies of Marilyn Monroe, if the term is used loosely to include picture books, anthologies of images, clippings and quotations, showcases for 'the legacy of her legend', sensational thrillers about the mystery of her death ('the evidence points to premeditated homicide'), feminist interpretations, fictional versions of her story, and sociological analyses of the construction of the 'star' and the commodification of the female body through the Hollywood system.

All versions promise a deeper, truer, more authentic Marilyn. All – typically of 'star biographies' – promise to get 'under the public image to the true life below' and to write about her 'as a human being, as opposed to a celluloid invention' even while recycling the gossip and reproducing the most famous images. Many speak of a special sense of affinity for their subject: 'I felt immediately drawn to her.' Almost all use her first name – either her real one, Norma Jeane/Jean, or her Hollywood name. All versions talk about childhood abuse and neglect, madness, rape, sex, beauty, the image of the 'dumb blonde', magnetism, charisma, pornography, Hollywood and the movie industry, publicity, fame, power, marriage, divorce, miscarriage, abortion, drugs, alcohol, self-destruction, fame, and death. There is no way of writing a Life of 'Marilyn' without dealing with these big topics, any more than without talking about Joe DiMaggio, Arthur Miller, or the Kennedy brothers. That is the attraction of the job: it is a big, symbolic American story.

All the biographies deal with her contradictions: natural and artificial, exhibitionistic and vulnerable, funny and tragic, dumb blonde and talented performer, desirable and frigid, sexually experienced and innocent-seeming, babyish and adult, mortal and immortal. An overview of such treatments, *The Many Lives of Marilyn Monroe* (2004), sees a shift over fifty years from 'sex symbol to symbol of mourning, from a promise of the liberation of sex to a cautionary tale about the dangers of loneliness'. The author, Sarah Churchwell, argues that the 'hidden' Marilyn is never to be found. The repeated dichotomies proposed by biography after biography – 'public/private, artifice/reality, fantasy/truth' – do not reveal a 'true' self: they reiterate a 'terminal either/or in which she is trapped'.

The most intensively interpretative versions, by three well-known American writers (Joyce Carol Oates, Norman Mailer, Gloria Steinem), all opt for the biographical theme of double identity. Norman Mailer read 'Marilyn', in his 1973 novel of that name, as both the ultimately desirable essence of Woman, described in lavish tumescent prose ('a cornucopia ... the angel of sex ... like a sweet peach bursting before one's eyes') and as a female Napoleon, an epic representative of archetypal human struggles. Joyce Carol Oates, in her fictional allegory of Eros and Thanatos, has 'Marilyn' as The Blonde who is pursued through her life by the Dark Prince and who is part smiling mask ('The Blonde Actress ... inhabiting her voluptuous body like a child crammed into a mannequin'), part abandoned 'unhappy little girl', always looking for her lost father.

The feminist writer Gloria Steinem's outraged lament for Monroe's tragic fate described her, in 1987, as split between the wretched, unloved Norma Jeane whom Marilyn spends her life trying to escape, and the public, artificially constructed Marilyn, who 'used her body as a gift to gain love and approval'. 'Whenever the public artifice failed and the private Norma Jeane seemed to be her only fate again . . . then depression and hopelessness took over . . . her body became her prison.' This protective elegy for Monroe as 'the emblematic female victim' may seem overly indulgent now, but its tone was in strong contrast to the locker-room ridicule and innuendo of many male treatments of the 'sex-goddess'. Anthony Summers's 1985 version was particularly snide: 'This need for a father figure seems to have become part of Marilyn's tapestry of fantasies'; 'One day Marilyn managed to break even her record for unpunctuality'; 'Marilyn now indulged her taste for intrigue and the ugly side of her temper'. The contrast in approaches points to more than differing treatments of one female superstar. It suggests biography's long-lasting tendency to treat exceptional and famous women differently from exceptional and famous men: not as 'role models' or admirable exemplars, but as freaks, warnings, objects of fear, desire, or ridicule, dangerous accidents, trouble-zones.

The two most famous and most reproduced images of 'Marilyn' are the publicity shot of her in the white dress blowing up over the subway vent (the huge entrancing smile, the amazing legs, the jokey sexiness, the mixture of natural life-force and urban sophistication, the exhibition for admiring onlookers) and the face as processed by another glamorous, short-lived media figure, Andy Warhol. Warhol's paintings of Marilyn, begun soon after her death in 1962, were part of his obsession with fame and violent early death, alongside Elvis with a gun and Jackie at the death of Kennedy. For *Marilyn Diptych* (1962), he used a cropped publicity photo which was enlarged and transferred to a silkscreen and became the basis for fifty identical images of Marilyn, laid out in ten regular blocks of five. On the left half of

17. Endless exposure: life flattened into myth

the diptych, the heads are coloured in lurid gold, pink, and blue. The right half is in black and white; some heads are heavily blotted with dark ink, some are fading out into nothingness. 'The row upon row of repeated heads call to mind postage stamps, bill board posters, but, perhaps, most of all . . . strips of film . . . both celebratory of a life and a mourning of a death.' Warhol's images of Monroe are the opposite of everything we want biography to be. They are flat, repetitive, banal, synthetic, journalistic, unrevealing. But they also offer a highly appropriate version of her life-story: endlessly exposed, instantly recognizable, unable to communicate anything except what has been constructed for public consumption. In that sense, they are the visual equivalent of a biography of a public life in the modern world, flattened irretrievably into myth.

Chapter 8
Telling the Story

'My God, how does one write a biography?' That was what
Virginia Woolf asked herself in 1938, while she was trying to write
a commissioned Life of her friend Roger Fry, and that was how
I began my biography of her in 1996. It seemed a suggestive way
in, since her life-story was already well known (so I didn't have to
start 'Adeline Virginia Stephen was born on the 25th January
1882') and she herself was so interested in, and so articulate
and sceptical about, biography and its conventions. I shaped her
life-story not entirely chronologically but partly by themes,
inspired by her own experimental novelistic strategies for accessing
the interior lives of her characters and dealing with time, memory,
and perspective. Any biographical narrative is an artificial
construct, since it inevitably involves selection and shaping.
No biographer is going to write down every single thing their
subject did, said, and thought on every day of their life from
birth to death, or the book would take longer than the life itself.
Given my subject's own interest in how life-stories can be told,
I decided to point up the artifice of the biographical narrative,
and to concentrate on particular aspects of the life, on different
'selves'. Other contemporary biographers are similarly
experimenting with form, building in an explicit commentary on
their own relation to the subject, using fictional strategies, or
playing with time and point of view.

There is an argument to be made against these sorts of experiments. Roy Foster, historian-biographer, faced with Yeats's mythologizing of his own life and its powerful after-effects on his biographers, wanted to 'restore the sense of a man involved in life, and in history: notably in the history of his country, at a time of exceptional flux and achievement'. '[Yeats's] *Autobiographies* dictates an arrangement for his life, and it is a thematic one . . . However, we do not, alas, live our lives in themes, but day by day; and WBY, giant though he was, is no exception.' Foster gets behind Yeats's commanding accounts of himself by use of steady chronological structure and massive investigative detail. But, in an admiring review of the biography, James Olney asks whether an undeviating chronological method, 'proceeding not by themes but day by day' is really possible. He cites Paul Valéry, wondering 'if anyone has ever tried to write a biography and attempted at each instant of it to know as little of the following moment as the hero of the work knew himself'. And he notes that Foster's biography 'commences in chronological record but then shades off into a fully interpretative and thematic narrative that is both retrospective and proleptic in its ordering'.

The examples of Woolf and Yeats suggest that different kinds of narrative may fit different kinds of biographical subjects. It would not have seemed helpful to experiment with form if I had been writing a Life of, say, Martin Luther King, or Ian Paisley, or Benazir Bhutto. In those cases, it would have been more useful to start with the history of American slavery and the Civil Rights movement, or with the tangled roots of Protestant Unionism in Northern Ireland, or with the Indo-Pakistan wars and the rise of the Bhutto dynasty. For political or historical biography, the form of the narrative may have to be steady and unsurprising, solid scaffolding for the blocks of facts.

As this book began by saying, there are no rules for telling a life-story. But there *are* some inevitable conventions. Whatever the story is about, whatever race, nationality, sex, class, language, or history is involved, there will have to be time, place, character, and events. Most biography moves forward and onward, sets the main figure in its context, mixes the plot with accounts of the subject's work, of historical complexities or of subsidiary characters, and uses description and observation, documentary sources, witness testimony, peripheral materials, and first-hand knowledge to construct the story. Biographers may choose to concentrate on a particular part of the life. They may start with a death, or a telling anecdote, or the subject's posthumous reputation, rather than with a birth. They may allow gaps and puzzles into the narrative, or try to smooth these over. They may introduce moral judgements or personal opinions. But they all want to give as full, intelligible, and accurate a version of the subject's life as possible. And they all want to make the specific facts and details add up to some overall idea of the subject, so that their biography, for the moment, will give the truest answer to the question: What was she, or he, like?

But even that basic list raises many alternative possibilities. My hypothetical Lives of King, Paisley, and Bhutto could have started differently: with a shot and a fall on the balcony of the Lorraine motel in Memphis in 1968; with an account of Ballymena, County Antrim, in the 1930s; with a description of the holy shrine that Bhutto's tomb, in her family mausoleum in Sindh province, has now become. Beginnings want to catch the reader's interest, of course, but they also set up the biographer's tone. Here are some examples:

'There will always be Shelley lovers, but this book is not for them.' Richard Holmes tells us in his first sentence that he is not going to be idolatrous or romanticizing, that he is writing against received versions, that he is bold and clear about his reasons for doing this, and that he knows that *his* Shelley will be one more version, not a definitive account.

'The story of Rebecca West (who lived from 1892 to 1983) is the story of twentieth-century women.' Victoria Glendinning lets us know at once, and firmly, why her subject matters, how she feels about it, and and what her approach is likely to be.

'It was the best of times and it was the worst of times. In the London household of Alexander and Edith Pope, Edith was expecting her first child.' The Pope scholar Maynard Mack, setting out on his magisterial 1985 Life of the poet, starts with an echo of Dickens which suggests that this is going to be a big historical story with the rich thick density of a 19th-century novel.

'On 1 February 1984, an Englishman with a rucksack and walking boots strides into a bungalow in the Irene district of Pretoria. He is six feet tall, with fair hair swept over a huge forehead and staring blue eyes. He is only a step ahead of the illness that will kill him. He is 45, but he has the animation of a schoolboy.' The present-tense beginning of Nicholas Shakespeare's Life of Bruce Chatwin promises a gripping adventure and a racy, intimate piece of reportage about a remarkable person.

'Decades after the blazing hot afternoon in June 1933 when Ralph Ellison, on his first and last outing as a hobo, climbed fearfully and yet eagerly aboard a smoky freight train leaving Oklahoma City on a dangerous journey that he hoped would take him to college in Tuskegee, Alabama, his memories of growing up in Oklahoma continued both to haunt and to inspire him. For a long time he had suppressed those memories, then the time came when he began to crave them.' This long-winded opening to Arnold Rampersad's Life of Ralph Ellison sets up a complicated interplay between past and present, aspiration and recollection. It tells us we are setting out on an exhaustive biographical journey, with a biographer who is in full possession of his subject's inner and outer life.

In each of these cases – and in any example you care to pick – the opening moves set up the whole approach. And this will vary depending on the subject. The biography of an unknown figure who has never been written about before may have to justify its existence, but can be free of the claims for specialness and slapping down of previous versions that biographies of much-covered figures may find necessary. Tone and approach will usually reveal whether this is an unknown subject, a resuscitation, an act of iconoclasm, an interim report on a living person, or a revisionist return, with new materials or the key to long-kept secrets, aiming to change our whole view of a well-known story.

Biography has a different job to do if it is dealing with what Virginia Woolf called 'lives of the obscure', than if it is retelling the story of Shakespeare or Napoleon. As biography is always involved with the social and cultural politics of its time and place, so its assumptions change about what is major or minor, permitted or shocking, mainstream or alternative. One striking example of biography's shifting standards is the recent popularity of 'group' biography (an ancient genre, newly revived), arising from an interest in democratizing a form that has tended to focus on single, dominant figures, and from a desire, in Jenny Uglow's phrase, 'to uncover a past we might otherwise miss'.

Such biographies may be about royal families or political dynasties, but they may also involve a challenge to the 'dominant discourse'. A feminist biographer working in the 1990s on the life of a working-class, Communist woman migrant to Australia raised the question of authority for biographers who choose 'alternative' subjects:

> The biographer who prefers to construct a version of history that is not, say, Captain Cook single-handedly appropriating Australia for British imperialism but, rather, the version of one of the sailors, or of one of the Aboriginal people who resisted the invasion, is presented with a wide range of problems. One of the central ones is: Who will speak?

Biographies that speak for alternative or hidden lives, especially women's – Jean Strouse on Henry James's sister Alice (1980),

Brenda Maddox on Joyce's wife Nora Barnacle (1988), Claire Tomalin on Dickens's mistress Ellen Ternan (1990), Alison Light on Virginia Woolf's servants (2007) – grow out of a feminist interest in 'hidden histories'. In *A Room of One's Own* (1929), Woolf imagined the many untold stories of women's lives, 'these infinitely obscure lives that still remain to be recorded'. Woolf's idea of what an unrecorded life might be, or how it might be told, would look different a hundred years on. As with biographies of African-American subjects, or native peoples, or lives set in post-colonial and developing nations, or queer and lesbian life-stories, or working-class histories, feminist biography (which may of course overlap with any of those other categories) is a changing genre, not a fixed entity.

This genre went through a period of reaction against historical assumptions about 'separate spheres', domestic priorities, modest invisibility, or aberrant exceptions. But female biography no longer needs to ask, as Carolyn Heilbrun did in the 1980s, what the story of a woman's life 'should look like', or to argue that 'biographies of women, if they have been written at all, have been written under the constraints of acceptable discussion'. The phase of disinterring obscure lives and of claiming new status and significance for women's stories – a process of consciousness-raising that has been described as 'critical to the feminist project of transforming the public sphere' – can now be spoken about in the past tense, as by the historian Carolyn Steedman, in *Past Tenses*: 'A sense of that which is lost, never to be recovered completely, has been one of the most powerful rhetorical devices of modern women's history.' (And, she adds, of working-class history.)

The telling of women's stories has often been talked about in terms of difference. Any account of female biography notes that: 'In truth, writing the lives of men and women *is* different... What is acceptable, what is possible, what is imagined and attempted often differ.' 'If biographies of men are dominated by external events, most biographies of women are a blend of external and internal.' 'It

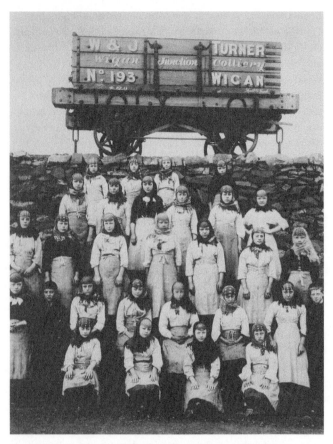

18. 'Pit Brow' girls: Group lives, women's lives, working lives

may be true that most women are still judged heavily by their private lives and men almost exclusively by their public.' If the subject is a writer, 'access to the privacy of the author seems more intensely desired when the author is a woman'. Women writers whose lives involved abuse, mental illness, self-harm, suicide, have often been treated, biographically, as victims or psychological case-histories first and as professional writers second. The agendas that surround such stories are acutely on view in biographies of Woolf or Plath, or, for instance, in Diane Wood Middlebrook's Life of the confessional American poet Anne Sexton, who killed herself, which made use of tapes of the subject talking to her analyst. Even if the various pitfalls in writing about women – personalizing, over-protectiveness, demonizing, punitiveness, condescension – have become much less common, the challenge remains of how best to tell the stories of the increasing numbers of women in the public sphere. 'It is still very difficult to account for women's influence and reputation in public arenas', writes one feminist critic, citing Steedman's biography of the early 20th-century socialist politician Margaret McMillan, which tried to find ways of lifting 'the dead weight of interiority that hangs about the neck of women's biography', and to tell the story of an entirely 'public life'.

A still lingering difference between biographies of men and of women is revealed by the matter of naming. Lives are no longer being written of 'Miss Austen', 'Mrs Woolf', or 'Mrs Gaskell'. But because biographies of women have for so long been more protective and intimate than those of great men, a biography of a famous English woman novelist might still refer throughout to Jane or Charlotte, while famous male English novelists are not usually called Charles or Anthony. Some biographers of women deal with this issue by switching from forename to surname, or from childhood nickname to married name, depending on whether early or later life, personal or professional matters, are being referred to. The *New Oxford DNB* has given this careful thought:

Evans, Marian [pseud. George Eliot] (1819–80), novelist, was known under several names during her life: Mary Anne Evans (at birth), Mary Ann Evans (from 1837), Marian Evans (from 1851), Marian Evans Lewes (from 1854), and Mary Ann Cross (1880).

George Eliot can be found, in the online version of the DNB, under any one of these names.

Naming is just one signal of the biography's approach to its subject. The construction of that approach begins with the book's cover, title, and contents page. These paratextual elements may be partly the work of the publisher rather than the author, but they set up expectations for a certain kind of narrative.

Lives of Jane Austen tend to have similar covers, because there is only one known portrait of her, drawn by her sister Cassandra. But the biography's approach will be suggested by whether the original, rather grumpy-looking, unromantic image is used, or the prettified, genteel version which was touched up by the next generation.

Titles tell a story, too. A biography called *Shakespeare: The Biography* makes a different kind of claim from *Will in the World: How Shakespeare became Shakespeare*, or *1599: A Year in the Life of William Shakespeare*. Contents pages are also part of the narrative. A biography of Keats that is simply divided up by numbered sections (and so has no chapters listed on its contents page) has a less prescriptive or novelistic air – but is harder to navigate – than one whose contents page has chapter titles such as 'Mr Keats's Origins', 'Sparks of the Divine', or 'The Death Warrant'. Some biographers (mostly European) divide their chapter titles up into sections, like indexes. So Jean-Yves Tadié's 1996 *Marcel Proust* has headings like 'Contre Sainte Beuve: Pastiches 504, Living for Writing 507, Financial Speculations and Virtuous Habits 509', giving the impression that the Life has been sliced up with utmost precision. Some biographers imitate their subject's manner in their chapter titles, as though pretending to be novelists. So Adrian Frazier's Life of the ebullient, self-dramatizing Irish novelist George Moore has chapters called 'Don Juan Jr in the Age of the National Vigilance Association', or 'Jesus of Nazareth and the Sage of Ebury Street'.

All those sorts of choices – the fullness or scarcity of footnotes, whether the index includes topics and concepts as well as names,

a

b

19. Miss Austen; Jane Austen; Jane . . .

the range and number of illustrations – are part of how the story is told and what kind of readership is envisaged: general or specialist, trade or academic. Length, too, tells us about the approach. Why was this subject thought worthy of 900 pages?

Or, why has a big subject been dealt with in 150 pages? What has been left out?

Biography's narrative tactics – often barely noticed as the facts unroll and the story moves on – set the tone and create a point of view. Narratives that go in for thunderous climaxes ('This was a watershed event in her life'), or dramatic summings-up ('Henry James chose the path of safety. He remained celibate'), or suspenseful anticipations – *he would come to regret this decision bitterly, things would never be the same again, from this moment she never looked back* – are, in Leon Edel's phrase, trying to 'borrow some of the techniques of fiction without lapsing into fictional biography'. Some biographers make free more blithely than others with their 'must haves' and 'might haves', their 'perhaps' and 'probablys'. Some approach their subject with a predetermined theory about what shaped their lives – illness, a family relationship, some form of damage or abuse – and make the story fit the theory. Some biographers use a great deal of description and scene-setting, and some make empathetic rather than factual portraits of their characters. This is a risky strategy, but can work well if the biographer is also a fiction writer, as in V. S. Pritchett's fine short Life of Turgenev:

> [Turgenev's mother] Varvara Petrovna's command of the passions, in all their manifestations, was inexhaustible. She was a round-shouldered woman with large, glaring black eyes under heavy brows, her forehead was wide and low, the skin of her face was coarse and pocked, her mouth large, sensual and cruel, her manner arrogant and capricious. She was as self-willed as a child, though like many ugly women she could be fascinating and charm her friends, and was very witty. Her history is pitiable.

The tone of voice used about the subject is a vital part of how the biographical story is told. Biographers sometimes ask themselves whether they think of their subject as younger or older than they are, in need of sympathetic protection or a daunting object of respect. Modern biographers often speak in a humorous, ironic, unshockable voice, making it clear that nothing human disgusts them. John Haffenden embarks on his mighty, and mightily peculiar, Life of William Empson with a reminiscence of having heard him read, inaudibly, at Trinity College Dublin in the 1960s:

> A woman cried out with exasperation from the back of the hall, 'Speak out, you silly old fool!' Whole rows of necks shrank into their shoulders with the embarrassment of it all, though later I was tipped off that the outspoken woman had been Empson's wife – so that was all right.

This cool comical tone is quite often used when sexuality is being described. Andrew Motion, detailing Larkin's interest in pornography, tells this story:

> Once, hesitating outside a shop in a funk, Larkin was approached by the owner who discreetly asked, 'Was it bondage, sir?'

Fiona MacCarthy, establishing her attitude to Eric Gill's sexual acts with (his) children and animals, writes bravely:

> Even his...practical experiments with bestiality, though they may strike one as bizarre, are not in themselves especially horrifying or amazing. Stranger things have been recorded.

More solemn biographical approaches turn their subjects' stories into archetypal tragedies, as in the conclusion to Michael Reynolds's epic biography of Hemingway:

> His is a classic American story: the young man who transforms himself following his ambition, succeeds beyond his dreams, and finally burns out trying to be true to the person he has become...It is an old story, older than written words, a story the ancient Greeks would have recognized.

Less sympathetic biographers use their subject as target-practice, and try to bring them down:

> Writers who posed a threat to Bellow's hegemony got the cold shoulder; writers who occupied a place safely below his own on the literary ladder were seen as comrades in the 'travail business', as Bellow liked to refer to his profession.

> Bellow ... inveighed against the unregulated sex of the permissive sixties while passing up no opportunity to indulge in it himself ... It was as if he hoped that his persistent moralizing could somehow neutralize his own libertine impulses – the ineffectual superego chastising the guilty id.

Biography is bound to incorporate the relationship of the writer and their subject, even if only subliminally. There is no such thing as an entirely neutral biographical narrative. Not everyone will agree with André Maurois that the main subject of any biography is 'the medium of the biographer's own feelings'. Not all biographers choose to say 'I'. Not all would want to identify their life with their subject's quite as closely as this psycho-biographer of Thoreau:

> In the past few years, my 'marriage' to Thoreau has evolved in new, unexpected directions ... Working ... on 'dialogues' between myself and Thoreau ... has revealed much to me about these directions in our relationship ... When I first worked on the dialogues, I had a sense, inspired by the possibility that my wife and I might be pregnant, that I was on the verge of a new period of my life. With the confirmation that we were indeed going to have a child, I have unquestionably entered a new phase ... I wonder now whether, or how, my relationship to Thoreau will be modified as I become involved in parenting ... I am hopeful that I can maintain and nurture an enduring I-Thou relationship with Thoreau.

Biography may, indeed, be a kind of marriage. If the biographer knows or has met their subject, their own feelings about them will colour the picture in some way. Selina Hastings's difficult friendship with Rosamond Lehmann, who became demanding and impatient with her biographer, shadowed her view of her. Samuel Beckett's characteristic response to his biographer Deirdre Bair – 'he would not help me, he said, but he would not hinder me, either' – left her free, but dogged by the feeling that 'he did not want this book to be written and would have been grateful if I had abandoned it'. Even when the biographer has not met their subject, they may find them resistant or obstructive, as Judith Thurman found Colette: 'She actively disdains all forms of empathy and resists being known.'

All biography is an attempt to take possession of the subject (A. S. Byatt's novels *Possession* and *The Biographer's Tale* deal passionately with this idea), but some biographers are more possessed – or possessive – than others. Some try to crawl right inside their skin, sleep in their beds, give their whole lives up to the pursuit. Norman Sherry, who tracked Graham Greene over many decades and volumes, put himself everywhere into the story, including illustrations of himself 'on the trail' of 'Our Man', to the point where Sherry seems to have become 'the virtual subject of the biography with Greene serving more as a vehicle for Sherry's self-portrayal than anything else'. Some biographers wrestle for years with rivals who believe that the subject belongs to them. Some take such masterful possession that they become forever associated with their subject; so we speak of Boswell's Johnson, Edel's James, Ellmann's Joyce. But biographers should beware, says Robert Graves:

> To bring the dead to life
> Is no great magic...
> Subdue your pen to his handwriting
> Until it prove as natural
> To sign his name as yours.
> Limp as he limped,
> Swear by the oaths he swore;

If he wore black, affect the same;

If he had gouty fingers,

Be yours gouty too.

Assemble tokens intimate of him –

A ring, a hood, a desk:

Around these elements then build

A home familiar to

The greedy revenant.

So grant him life, but reckon

That the grave which housed him

May not be empty now:

You in his spotted garments

Shall yourself lie wrapped.

Biographers who are totally in possession, who know everything there is to know, have different kinds of narrative problems from biographers who know too little. Shakespeare is the obvious example. His many biographers differ widely – or wildly – in their lines of approach, between romantic guesswork, dogged sleuthing, historical contextualizing, postmodernist indeterminacy. Two 21st-century examples illustrate the range of possibilities. Charles Nicholl quests like a detective, through the record of a 1612 court case at which Shakespeare gave evidence, into the time he spent living in a house in Cripplegate, where he was known as 'merely the lodger, the gent in an upstairs chamber: a certain Mr Shakespeare'. Tracking Shakespeare down to Silver Street involves the close reading of a few scattered clues, guesswork, and invention: the result is the opening of 'an unexpected little window into Shakespeare's life'. By contrast, Jonathan Bate takes a broad, sweeping, inclusive approach in *Soul of the Age*, a masterly intellectual biography of Shakespeare, constructed not strictly chronologically, but on the basis of the 'seven ages of man', to reveal what he refers to as Shakespeare's cultural DNA.

James Shapiro, in his 'micro-biography' of a year in Shakespeare's life, argues that to read back from the works into Shakespeare's feelings, as if the plays were a 'two-way mirror', ends in 'circularity and arbitrariness'. But there is a great temptation for Shakespeare's biographers to make as much as they can of the little they know. Take one of the many baffling and obscure facts of Shakespeare's life, the death of his son Hamnet at the age of 11 in 1596, about which Shakespeare made no recorded utterance. The closeness of the names Hamnet and Hamlet, and the fact that Shakespeare played the Ghost of Hamlet's father, has led to a wealth of quasi-fictional speculations, from Stephen Dedalus's theories of fatherhood in Joyce's *Ulysses* to Anthony Burgess's blithe claim, in a popular 1970 picture book on the Bard, that 'Shakespeare transmuted his own son into a mad Danish prince'. In Shapiro's biography, Hamnet's death is treated as follows. He works out exactly where Shakespeare would have been (on tour) when he heard the news in August 1596; he tells us which Stratford carrier would have brought him the news, and what that carrier's knowledge of Shakespeare was. He establishes that Shakespeare would not have had time to get home for the funeral, and he tells us how little Shakespeare knew his son and how rarely he saw him. 'Which is not to say', Shapiro adds, 'that he did not feel his loss deeply. It may even have accounted for his diminished output in the year or so that followed. We just don't know.' When he discusses *Hamlet*, he deals minutely with the play's textual versions, ethics, cultural references, production, performance, and reception, but says nothing about the play's possible relation to Shakespeare's dead son.

Other biographers take different tones. Park Honan's 1998 Life methodically tracks all the known facts and received opinions back to their sources, and describes itself as 'dispassionate', yet still allows itself a little emotional guesswork. From the evidence of Shakespeare's work after 1596, Honan supposes that the death of Hamnet 'changed him', that 'he seems never to have recovered from the loss', and that it 'deepened him as an artist and thinker'. Honan's speculations are mild, though, compared with Stephen Greenblatt's in his bold, popular *Will in the World: How*

Shakespeare became Shakespeare (2004). Greenblatt jumps from saying that 'there is, at the very least, no reason to think that Shakespeare simply buried his son and moved on unscathed', to a full-blown hypothesis about the 'deep wound reopening', leading to 'a crisis of mourning and memory', 'a psychic disturbance that may help to explain the explosive power and inwardness of *Hamlet*'. Not for Greenblatt the words 'we just don't know'. Peter Ackroyd's 2005 biography does more hedging of bets:

> So Shakespeare had lost his only son ... It is of course impossible to gauge the effect upon the dramatist. He may, or may not, have become inconsolable. He may have sought refuge, as so many others have done, in hard and relentless work. The plays of this period have nevertheless been interpreted in the light of this dead son ... Indeed it cannot be wholly coincidental that Shakespeare was drawn at a later date to the tragedy of Hamlet.

All biographers have at times to suppose and infer. If their research is good and their sense of the subject is strong, then their guesses will be worth listening to. Purists would argue, though, that there are things that biography ought to leave to fiction, or to biopics like *Shakespeare In Love* or *Becoming Jane*: imaginary conversations, invented dreams and fantasies, emotional crises for which there is no evidence, unproven psychic traumas. For all biography's efforts to place the fish in the stream, to provide detailed material texture, cultural contextualizing, and social particularity, to go as far as it can in the interpretation of character, there will always, also, be areas of obscurity and absence. Biographers may – and probably ought to – end their work still feeling that there were many things they never discovered.

There is often a wistful note on the last page of biographies, as though the end of the task is also the end of a relationship. Biographers find it hard to narrate the deaths of their subjects without any emotion, as simply the next and final event in the

Ex dono Will: Jaggard Typographi a° 1623

MR. WILLIAM
SHAKESPEARES
COMEDIES,
HISTORIES, &
TRAGEDIES.

Published according to the True Originall Copies.

Martin Droeshout sculpsit London

LONDON
Printed by Isaac Iaggard, and Ed. Blount. 1623.

20. William Shakespeare?

story. Most biographers feel the need to make some gesture of farewell. The final stage of writing a biography is separation and letting go, and the recognition that the version that has been constructed is bound to be partial and temporary. At the end of all the labour of reconstruction and representation, the biographer is left looking at the receding view of the person they have been obsessed with, moving away from them into the silence of the past.

References

Chapter 1: The Biography Channel

P. 2

Henry James to Harry James (1915), *Henry James: Letters*, ed. Leon Edel (Harvard University Press), Vol. IV, p. 806, quoted in Ian Hamilton (1992), p. 220. Shakespeare's epitaph: 'Good Frend For Jesus Sake Forbeare,/To Digg The Dust Encloased Heare!/Blest Be Ye Man Yt Spares Thes Stones,/And Curst be He Yt Moves My Bones.'

P. 3

For Hazlitt on portraits, see Wendorf (1990), p. 7. For Plutarch, see 'Life of Alexander', in *Greek Lives*, tr. R. Waterfield (Oxford University Press, 1998), p. 312. For Boswell on portraits, see Wendorf (1990), p. 260, and Redford (2002), pp. 57–64.

Keats, *Letter to George and Georgiana Keats*, 19 March 1819, *The Letters of John Keats*, ed. H. E. Rollins (Harvard University Press, 1958), Vol. II, p. 80.

'Light gleams': Carlyle, Review of Croker's edition of Boswell's *Life of Johnson*, April 1832, in Clifford (1962), pp. 82, 83.

P. 4

'Biographical subjects...': Wendorf (1990), p. 13.

P. 5

For definitions of 'biography', see the *New Oxford Thesaurus of English* (2000), the OED of 1971 and the New OED of 2001.

For postmortems, see Stefan Timmermans, *Postmortem; How Medical Examiners Explain Suspicious Deaths* (University of Chicago Press, 2006).

P. 6

Jenny Uglow, *The Lunar Men* (Faber, 2002); Megan Marshall, *The Peabody Sisters: Three Women Who Ignited American Romanticism* (Houghton Mifflin, 2006).

P. 7

John Updike, *New York Review of Books*, 4 February 1999, quoted in France and St Clair (2002), p. 8.

P. 8

Alethea Hayter, *A Sultry Month: Scenes of London Literary Life in 1846* (Faber, 1965); David Edmonds and John Eidinow, *Wittgenstein's Poker* (Faber, 2001); James Shapiro, *1599: A Year in the Life of William Shakespeare* (Faber, 2005), p. xx.

P. 9

Biography

For 'public sphere', see Jürgen Habermas, *The Structural Transformation of the Public Sphere*, tr. T. Burger and F. Lawrence (Polity Press, 1989).

'Saints' Lives': Jocelyn Wogan-Browne and Glyn Burgess (eds.), *Virgin Lives and Holy Deaths* (Everyman, 1996), p. xvi.

'Social Intercourse': Boswell, *Life*, 31 March 1772, cited in Clifford (1962), p. 47.

'Autobiography': E.g. Maurois (1929), p. 112, on biography as 'disguised autobiography'; Phyllis Rose, in Rhiel and Suchoff (1996), p. 131, on biography as a form of autobiography.

'Broken bridge': Holmes (1985, 1995), p. 27.

John Donne, 'Meditation XVII', in *Devotions Upon Emergent Occasions* (1624), *John Donne: Complete Poetry and Selected Prose* (Nonesuch Library, 1955), p. 538.

Thomas Carlyle, review of Lockhart's *Life of Scott*, *The London and Westminster Review*, January 1838, in Clifford (1962), pp. 84–5.

Virginia Woolf, 'Sketch of the Past', *Moments of Being* (1985; Pimlico, 2002), p. 90.

'Status quo': Holroyd, in Homberger and Charmley (1988), p. 98.

P. 10

J.-P. Sartre, *L'Idiot de la Famille: Gustave Flaubert de 1821 à 1857* (Paris, 1988); John Gibson Lockhart, *Memoirs of the Life of Sir Walter Scott* (Edinburgh, 1837); Leon Edel, *Henry James: A Life* (Harper & Row, 1985).

'Unauthorized': E.g. Carole Klein, 'There are a great many others who would only speak to me on promise of anonymity'. 'Acknowledgements', *Doris Lessing: A Biography* (Duckworth, 2000), p. vii.

'Secrecy': E.g. Victoria Glendinning, *Elizabeth Bowen: Portrait of a Writer* (Weidenfeld & Nicolson, 1977), cites love-letters between Bowen and Humphry House, given to the biographer by Humphry House's widow on condition that he should not be named. The paperback (Penguin, 1985), published after Madeline House's death, identifies him.

P. 11

Johnson, *The Rambler*, 60, 13 October 1750, in Clifford (1962), pp. 40–3.

Chapter 2: Exemplary Lives

P. 19

Moses: 'The Book of Deuteronomy', *Old Testament*, Authorized Version, Ch. 34, verses 4–8.

Socrates: Plato, *Phaedo*, tr. David Gallop (Oxford University Press, 1993, 1999), p. 77.

Alexander: Plutarch, 'Life of Alexander', in *Greek Lives*, tr. R. Waterfield (Oxford University Press, 1998), p. 323.

P. 20

Jesus: 'The Gospel according to St Matthew', *New Testament*, Authorized Version, Ch. 26, verses 38–41.

Caligula: Suetonius, 'Caligula', *Lives of the Caesars*, tr. Catharine Edwards (Oxford University Press, 2000), p. 165.

Jerome: 'St Jerome and the Lion', Yale University MS Beinecke 317, reprinted in Gordon Whatley, Anne Thompson, and Robert Upchurch (eds.), *Saints' Lives in Early Middle English Collections*, Middle English Text Series (2004), p. 147.

PP. 20–1

Old Testament narrative: see Erich Auerbarch, *Mimesis*, tr. Willard Trask (1953; Doubleday, 1957), Ch. 1, 'Odysseus's Scar'.

P. 22

Gilgamesh and Egyptians: see Nigel Hamilton (2007), pp. 13–17; Parke (2002), pp. 1–2.

P. 23

Plutarch, 'Life of Pericles', 'Life of Alcibiades', 'Life of Alexander', in *Greek Lives*, pp. 145, 242, 312. For Plutarch as moralist and biographer, see Christopher Pelling, *Plutarch and History* (Duckworth, 2002), esp. Ch. 10, 'The Moralism of Plutarch's Lives'; Pelling (ed.), *Characterisation and Individuality in Greek Literature* (Oxford University Press, 1990); Timothy Duff, *Plutarch's Lives* (Oxford University Press, 1999), and Reed Whittemore, *Pure Lives: The Early Biographers* (Johns Hopkins, 1983), pp. 4–26.

'Lasting influence': see J. W. Smeed, *The Theophrastian 'Character': The History of a Literary Genre* (Clarendon Press, 1985); Judith Mossman, 'Plutarch and English Biography', *Hermathena* (2007), No. 183: 71–96.

P. 24

Dryden: Preface to the *Lives of Plutarch*, 1683.

'Hagiography': Gordon Whatley, *op. cit.*, p. 2.

'Prototypical virtues': see Sergei Averintsev, 'From Biography to Hagiography', in France and St Clair (2002), pp. 19–36.

'Hagiography…dominant': Sherry L. Reames, *Middle English Legends of Women Saints* (Kalamazoo, 2003), p. 1.

PP. 24–5

Later hagiographies: Mrs John Sandford, *Lives of English Female Worthies* (Longmans, 1883); Gamaliel Bradford, *Saints and Sinners* (Kennikut Press, 1931); Evelyn Waugh, *Edmund Campion* (Longmans, 1935); Kathryn Spink, *Mother Theresa: An Authorised Biography* (HarperCollins, 1997); Jose Luis Gonzalez-Balado, *Mother Theresa: Her Life, Her Work, Her Message* (Hodder & Stoughton, 1997); Anne Sebba, *Mother Theresa: Beyond the Image* (Weidenfeld & Nicolson, 1997); David Lewis, *Martin Luther King: A Critical Biography* (Allen Lane, 1970); Valerie Schloredt, *Martin Luther King: America's Great Non-Violent Leader* (Exley, 1988); David J. Garrow, *Bearing the Cross: Martin Luther King and the Southern Christian Leadership Conference* (William Morrow, 1986).

P. 26

St Catherine: Sherry L. Reames, *op. cit.*; Jocelyn Wogan-Browne, *Virgin Lives and Holy Deaths* (Everyman, 1996), pp. 3–42; Karen Winstead, 'Saintly Exemplarity', in *Middle English: Oxford 21st Century Approaches to Literature*, ed. Paul Strohm (Oxford University Press, 2007), pp. 335–46.

Saints' Lives: Winstead, *op. cit.*, pp. 338, 346; Wogan-Browne, *op. cit.*, p. xiii. See also Anne Thompson, *Everyday Saints and the Art of Narrative in the South England Legendary* (Ashgate, 2005), and Thomas J. Heffernan, *Sacred Biography* (Oxford University Press, 1988).

P. 28

Worthies: Thomas Fuller, *Worthies of England* (1662; ed. J. Nichols, London, 1811).

Edmund Gosse: 'Biography', *Encylopaedia Britannica*, 11th edition (1910–11), pp. 952–3.

Attacks on hagiography: Kendall (1965), pp. 41, 59; Parke (2002), p. 7; Nigel Hamilton (2007), p. 57. Reames, *op. cit.*, p. 2.

P. 29

Lydgate: Stauffer (1930), pp. 28–9; *The Mirour for Magistrates*, ed. Lily B. Campbell (Cambridge University Press, 1938).

Alexander: Richard Stoneman (ed.), *Legends of Alexander the Great* (Everyman, 1994).

P. 30

'Rhetorical performances': Debora Shuger, 'Life-Writing in Seventeenth-Century England', in Coleman, *op. cit.*, p. 73.

Francis Bacon: *The Advancement of Learning*, in *The Major Works*, ed. Brian Vickers (Oxford University Press, 2002), pp. 180–2. Cited in Altick (1965), p. 8; Parke (2002), p. 13, and many other books on biography.

'Dangerous': see Shelston (1977), pp. 18–19; Nigel Hamilton (2007), pp. 70–4.

Cavendish: see Stauffer (1930), pp. 123–9; Anderson (1984), Ch. 3.

Sir Thomas More, *History of Richard III* (1557; Hesperus, 2005), p. 55. See Anderson (1984), pp. 78–92.

Walpole: cited in Pat Rogers, 'Introduction', Boswell's *Life of Johnson* (Oxford University Press, World's Classics, 1980) [hereafter *Life*], p. xxiv.

Macaulay: Review of 'Croker's Edition of Boswell's *Life of Johnson*', *Edinburgh Review*, 54 (September 1831): 1–38.

For Boswell's writing of the *Life*, see Sisman (2000), and Redford (2002). For Boswell's works, see *The Yale Editions of the Private Papers of James Boswell*. For Johnson separated from Boswell, see Donald Greene (ed.), *Samuel Johnson* (Oxford University Press, 1984); Norma Clarke, *Dr Johnson's Women* (Hambledon & London, 2000); Holmes (1993). Roger Lonsdale (ed.), *Johnson's The Lives of the Poets*, 4 vols (Oxford University Press, 2006).

'Pickling': *Life*, pp. 862, 297.

French 'ana': Jefferson (2007), pp. 36 ff.

Margaret, Duchess of Newcastle, *The Life of William Cavendish, Duke of Newcastle* (1667; ed. C. H. Firth, Routledge, 1907). Pepys on Cavendish, 18 March 1668, in *The Diary of Samuel Pepys: A New and Complete Transciption*, ed. Roberth Latham and William Matthews, vol. 9 (1668–9; G. Bell & Sons Ltd, 1976), p. 123.

Lucy Hutchinson, *Memoir of Colonel Hutchinson* (1664; Longmans, 1810). Margaret Oliphant, *Blackwood's Edinburgh Magazine*, July 1882, quoted in Marcus (1994), p. 46.

P. 31

William Roper, *The Life of Sir Thomas More* (Early English Text Society, Oxford University Press, 1935), pp. 83, 102.

17th-century French biography: see Jefferson (2007), pp. 31–9, and Peter France, 'The French Academic *Eloge*', in France and St Clair (2002), Ch. 5.

Italian biography: see Martin McLaughlin, 'Biography and Autobiography in the Italian Renaissance', in France and St Clair (2002), Ch. 3.

'Memoirs, diaries...': Shuger, *op. cit.*, p. 63.

PP. 34–5

Johnson's *Lives*, ed. Lonsdale: panegyric, 'Cowley', vol. I, p. 191; actions, 'Cowley', vol. I, p. 198; 'Milton', vol. I, p. 276. On Johnson's irony, Lonsdale, 'Introduction', p. 98.

PP. 34–6

Walton: see Jessica Martin, *Walton's Lives* (Oxford University Press, 2001), pp. 132, 169, 311, 315, and *passim*; Wendorf (1990), Ch. 2; Anderson (1984); David Novarr, *The Making of Walton's Lives* (Ithaca, 1958; Epstein, 1987), Ch. 2.

P. 36

Johnson's talk: *Life*, pp. 444, 1285, 343. 'Very uncivil', *Life*, p. 864.

'Newborn child': *Life*, p. 421. Leslie Stephen, *Samuel Johnson* (Macmillan, 1878), p. 90.

PP. 36–8

'Skediasmata': Anthony Powell, *John Aubrey and His Friends* (Eyre & Spottiswoode, 1948), p. 127.

John Aubrey to Anthony Wood, 15 June 1680, in *Aubrey's Brief Lives*, ed. Oliver Lawson Dick (Secker & Warburg, 1949), p. cxiii.

Chapter 3: Warts and All

P. 39

'We danced . . .': Boswell, *Journal of a Tour to the Hebrides*, [hereafter *Tour*], 1785, 'Sunday 2 October 1773'.

P. 42

'Assiduous enquiry': *Tour*, 'Thursday 14 October 1773'.

P. 46

Boswell in trouble: see Sisman (2000), Ch. 6.

'Wens and warts': Elizabeth Montagu to Hester Thrale [Piozzi], quoted Clifford, 'How Much Should a Biographer Tell?', in Daghlian (1968), p. 87.

PP. 46–7

'Conversation': *Life*, p. 23. 'Authenticity': quoted Sisman (2000), p. 114. 'Minute particulars': *Life*, p. 25.

P. 47

Roger North: see Clifford (1962), pp. xii, 27–37, and Wendorf (1990), pp. 152–4.

Johnson's essays, in Clifford (1962), pp. 40–3. First OED citation of 'autobiography', Robert Southey (1809).

PP. 47–8

Savage: Holmes (1993).

'Instructive detachment': Roger Lonsdale, 'Introduction', Johnson's *The Lives of the Poets*, vol. I (Oxford University Press, 2006), p. 85.

P. 48

Addison: *The Freeholder*, No. 35, 20 April 1716, in Clifford (1962), p. 25.

PP. 48–9

Curll: see Paul Baines and Pat Rogers, *Edmund Curll: Bookseller* (Oxford University Press, 2007). Arbuthnot's remark, often

misquoted as 'he adds a new terror to Death', is made in 1733 in a
letter to Swift about Curll's forthcoming life of Gay.

P. 49

'Flemish picture': Boswell, *Journal*, 1775, from *Boswell: The Ominous
Years, 1774–1776*, ed. C. Ryskamp and F. A. Pottle (Heinemann,
1963), p. 103, cited Wendorf (1990), p. 266, in a full account of
Boswell's use of portraiture. 'Act of looking', Redford (2002), p. 15.
Johnson's appearance: *Life*, pp. 280, 105, 330, 342, 1212.

PP. 50–1

'Jack Wilkes': *Life*, pp. 764–76. See Redford (2002), pp. 104–9. Jack
Ketch was a famous hangman.

P. 50

Johnson's sayings: *Life*, pp. 299, 1023, 435, 777, 400, 1217.

P. 51

Johnson's heroism: *Life*, pp. 416, 427.
Johnson's sentiment: *Life*, pp. 359, 1210.
Johnson's stoicism: *Life*, pp. 328, 240.

P. 53

'He disappeared': *Life*, p. 334.

Chapter 4: National Biography

P. 54

'Self-fashioning': Lucy Newlyn, *Coleridge, Wordsworth and the
Language of Allusion* (1986), Preface to the Second Edition (Oxford
University Press, 2000), p. xv, citing Stephen Greenblatt.
Herder: see Park Honan (1990), p. 28, on the importance of Herder's
On the Origin of Language (1772) for the development of life-
writing.

P. 55

'Boswell Redivivus': Hazlitt, *Conversations of James Northcote*, 1826–7,
in *The Collected Works of William Hazlitt* (Dent, 1903), vol. VI,
Notes, p. 505.
'Minutiae': Coleridge, *The Friend* (1850), II, p. 225, in Altick (1965),
p. 193.
James Field Stansfield: *An Essay on the Study and Composition of
Biography* (Sunderland, 1813), pp. 14, 21, 26.

PP. 55-6

Coleridge: Hazlitt, 'Mr Coleridge', in *The Spirit of the Age*, 1824–5; compare with 'My First Acquaintance with Poets', 1823. See also on Coleridge's conversation, Virginia Woolf, 'The Man at the Gate', 1940, *Collected Essays*, ed. Leonard Woolf (Chatto & Windus, 1966–7), vol. IV, pp. 117–21, and Seamus Perry, 'The Talker', *Cambridge Companion to Coleridge* (2002), pp. 103–25. Carlyle, *The Life of John Sterling* (Chapman & Hall, 1851), pp. 69–71.
'Human soul': Carlyle, *op. cit.*, p. 8.

P. 57

'Open loving heart': Carlyle, Review of Croker's edition of Boswell's *Life*, *Fraser's Magazine*, April 1832, in Clifford (1962), pp. 78–83.
'Damocles' sword': Carlyle, Review of Lockhart's *Life of Scott*, *The London and Westminster Review*, January 1838, in Clifford (1962), pp. 85–6.
'Outcry': John Gibson Lockhart, *Life of Robert Burns* (Edinburgh, 1828), p. 227, in Cockshut (1974), p. 27. Ian Hamilton (1992), p. 117. Altick (1965), p. 238. Richard Holmes, *Shelley: The Pursuit* (Weidenfeld & Nicolson, 1974; Quartet Books, 1976), pp. x–xi.

P. 58

'Johnson's brother': F. W. Maitland, *The Life and Letters of Leslie Stephen* (Duckworth & Co., London, 1906), pp. 419–20.

P. 59

Gaskell's Brontë: Elizabeth Gaskell, *The Life of Charlotte Brontë* (1857; Everyman, ed. J. Uglow, 1992), p. 245. Jenny Uglow, *Elizabeth Gaskell: A Habit of Stories* (Faber, 1993), p. 406.

PP. 61-2

On Gaskell's Brontë: Heilbrun (1988), p. 22. Heather Glen, *Charlotte Brontë: The Imagination in History* (Oxford University Press, 2002), pp. 274–6. Margaret Oliphant, quoted in Jenny Uglow, *Elizabeth Gaskell*, pp. 391, 407. Christopher Ricks, 'E. C. Gaskell's Charlotte Brontë', *Essays in Appreciation* (Oxford University Press, 1996), p. 145.

P. 62

Eccentrics: see James Gregory, 'Eccentric Biography and the Victorians', *Biography*, 30.3 (2007): 342–76. In France, Gérard de Nerval specialized in biographies of eccentrics; see Jefferson (2007), Ch. 9. For oddities in the DNB, see Keith Thomas on eccentrics, *Changing Conceptions of National Biography*

(Oxford University Press, 2004), pp. 22–4. For English
eccentricity, see also Virginia Woolf, 'The Eccentrics', 1919,
Collected Essays, vol. III, p. 29.

P. 63

'Reticence': Gladstone on Cross, in Kathryn Hughes, *George Eliot: The
Last Victorian* (Fourth Estate, 1998), p. 485.

Death-beds: John Morley, *Life of Gladstone* (Macmillan, 1903), p. 528.
John Wolffe, *Good Deaths* (Oxford University Press, 2000), p. 158.
Lee (2005, 2008), p. 202.

Nelson: Robert Southey, *Life of Nelson* (John Murray, [1813], 1832),
p. 296.

P. 64

Biographical dictionaries: Nadel (1984), p. 47. Jefferson (2007), pp. 83–5.
Keith Thomas, *op. cit.* (2005), p. 15. G. F. Watts (1887), cited in Peter
Funnell, *Victorian Portraits in the National Portrait Gallery
Collection* (NPG Publications, 1996), p. 4. Parke (2002), Ch. 5.

P. 65

'The lives of women': Mrs John Sandford, *Lives of English Female
Worthies* (Longmans, 1883), vol. I, pp. ix–x.

Samuel Smiles: *Self-Help* (1859; Oxford University Press, 2002),
pp. 20, 29.

P. 66

'Saints' legends': Richard Altick, *The English Common Reader* (1957;
Ohio State University Press, 1998), p. 242.

'Polemical agenda': David Amigoni, *Victorian Biography* (Harvester,
1993).

DNB: Leslie Stephen, 'A New *Biographia Britannica*', *Athenaeum*,
23 December 1882, in Novarr (1986), pp. 1–2. See Ian
Donaldson, 'National Biography', in France and St Clair
(2002), pp. 78–80. Sidney Lee, 'The Leslie Stephen Lecture', May
1911, published as *Principles of Biography*, 1911; Leslie Stephen
to Norman Moore, 1884, both quoted in Nadel (1984), pp. 54–6.
Leslie Stephen, 'National Biography', March 1896, *Studies of
a Biographer* (Duckworth, 1898), vol. 1, pp. 21–2. Keith
Thomas, *op. cit.* (2005), pp. 23, 45. Gillian Fenwick, *Women
and the DNB* (Aldershot, 1994), calculated that of the
28,201 entries in the DNB and its 31,901 supplements,
998 were on women. The Oxford DNB (2004) raised the
proportion to 10%.

P. 67

'Missing persons': C. S. Nicholls, 'Preface', *Missing Persons Supplement to the DNB* (Oxford University Press, 1993), pp. vi–vii. See also Robert Faber and Brian Harrison, 'The DNB: A Publishing History', *Lives in Print*, eds. Robin Myers, Michael Harris, and Giles Mandelbrote (Oak Knoll Press and British Library, 2002), pp. 171–92.

PP. 67–8

'Oblivion': Leslie Stephen, 'Forgotten Benefactors', 1895, in *Social Rights and Duties: Addresses to Ethical Societies*, 2 vols (Macmillan, 1896), II, p. 225. George Eliot, *Middlemarch* (1871–2), Finale.

P. 68

'Squalor': Jefferson (2007), Ch. 4.

PP. 68–9

On exposure: Browning, 'House', 1876. Tennyson, 'After Reading a Life and Letters' [of Keats], *The Examiner*, 24 March 1849. Ian Hamilton (1992), p. 181. George Eliot, Letter to Mrs Thomas Trollope, 19 December 1879, *The George Eliot Letters*, ed. Gordon Haight, vol. 7 (Oxford University Press and Yale University Press, 1956), p. 230. Thackeray, in Henrietta Garnett, *Anny: A Life of Anne Thackeray Ritchie* (Chatto, 2004), p. 265.

P. 69

James: Henry James to Edith Wharton, 13 March 1912, p. 215, in Hermione Lee, *Edith Wharton* (Chatto & Windus, 2007), p. 227. Henry James to Edmund Gosse, 8 April 1895, in Philip Horne (ed.), *Henry James: A Life in Letters* (Allen Lane, 1999), p. 279. Henry James, Review of William Ellery Channing's correspondence (1875), in Richard Salmon, 'The Right to Privacy/The Will to Knowledge', in Gould and Staley (1998), pp. 135–49, and Salmon, *Henry James: the Culture of Publicity* (Cambridge University Press, 1997). Ian Hamilton (1992), pp. 207–8.

'Ethics': Margaret Oliphant, 'The Ethics of Biography', *Contemporary Review*, July 1883, XLIV: 76–93, in Clifford (1962), pp. 97–102.

P. 70

Froude/Carlyle: J. A. Froude, *My Relations with Carlyle* (J. Lane, 1903). Sir James Crichton-Browne, *British Medical Journal* 27 June 1903: 1498, in Broughton, (1999), p. 140. See Elinor Shaffer, 'Shaping Victorian Biography', in France and St Clair (2002), pp. 115–33, and Altick (1965), Ch. 7.

P. 71

'The world has no business': Carlyle, *Journal*, 10 October 1843, in
   Origo (1984), p. 1.

Chapter 5: Fallen Idols

P. 72

Shaw: in Holroyd (2002), p. 25.

'Clumsy and laborious': Virginia Woolf, 'The New Biography', *Collected
   Essays* (Chatto & Windus, 1966–7), vol. 4. For 'Victorians', see also
   Strachey (1918, 2003), 'Preface'; Nicolson (1928); Kendall (1965),
   p. 105; Holroyd, in Homberger and Charmley (1988), p. 98; Nigel
   Hamilton (2007), Ch. 4.

'Marionette': Evelyn Waugh, *Rossetti: His Life and Works* (Duckworth,
   1928), p. 12.

PP. 73–5

'Fish in the stream': Virginia Woolf, 'Sketch of the Past', *Moments of
   Being* (Pimlico, 2003), p. 92.

P. 75

Gosse: Edmund Gosse, 'Preface', *Father and Son: A Study of Two
   Temperaments* (Heinemann, 1907). Evan Charteris, *The Life and
   Letters of Sir Edmund* Gosse (Heinemann, 1931), p. 305. See Lee
   (2005, 2008), pp. 100–11, and Ann Thwaite's biographies of
   Edmund Gosse (1984) and Philip Gosse (2002).

PP. 75–6

Strachey: John Sutherland, 'Introduction', *Eminent Victorians* (Oxford
   University Press World's Classics, 2003), p. x. Strachey (1918,
   2003), 'Preface', pp. 5–6, 162, 98, 201.

P. 77

'Condescension': Origo (1984), p. 21.

P. 78

Gosse: Edmund Gosse, 'Biography' (1911), pp. 952–3; Gosse (1925),
   pp. 8, 14.

Schwob: see Jefferson (2007), pp. 206–9.

New biography: Nicolson (1928). See Edel (1959, 1973), pp. 6–7;
   Marcus, in France and St Clair (2002), pp. 199–200; Hoberman
   (1987), Ch. 3.

P. 79

Maurois (1929). See Jefferson (2007), pp. 221, 224–5; Marcus, *op. cit.*, pp. 200–1.

Ludwig: see Marcus (1994), p. 131, and Altick (1965), p. 289.

Gamaliel Bradford: 'Confessions of a Biographer', in *Wives* (Harper & Bros, 1925), p. 12, and *A Naturalist of Souls* (Houghton Mifflin, 1926), pp. 5–8, quoted Marcus, in France and St Clair (2002), p. 207.

PP. 80–1

Woolf: 'The New Biography' (1927), 'The Art of Biography' (1939) in *Collected Essays* (Chatto & Windus, vol. 4). See also her 'An Unwritten Novel', 'The Genius of Boswell', 'A Talk about Memoirs', 'Walter Sickert', and see Hermione Lee, *Virginia Woolf* (Chatto & Windus, 1996), Ch. 1, 'Biography'. *Orlando* (1928; Penguin, 1993), p. 213.

P. 82

Zélide: Richard Holmes (ed.), *Scott on Zélide* (Harper Perennial Classic Biographies, 2004).

Corvo: A. J. A. Symons, *The Quest for Corvo: An Experiment in Biography* (Cassell, 1934, 1955), p. 219. See Marcus in France and St Clair (2002), pp. 211–14; Epstein (1987), pp. 170–1.

PP. 84–6

Freud: Freud to Strachey, 1928, Marcus, in France and St Clair (2002), p. 216. Adam Phillips, 'The Death of Freud', *Darwin's Worms* (Faber, 1999), pp. 85, 88, 93, 107. *Leonardo Da Vinci and a Memory of Childhood* (1910), pp. 50–3, 99, in *The New Penguin Freud*, ed. Adam Phillips; *The Uncanny*, tr. David McLintock (Penguin, 2003), Hugh Haughton, 'Introduction', pp. xxix, xxxvii. Freud followed a German mistranslation, 'vulture', for the Italian word 'nibio', 'kite', leading him to an interpretation of Leonardo's memory of 'a vulture putting its tail into his baby mouth' as 'a coded homosexual fantasy of oral sex'. See also Malcolm Bowie, 'Freud and the Art of Biography', in France and St Clair (2002), pp. 187–8.

P. 86

Freud's influence: Anthony Storr, *Freud* (Oxford University Press Past Masters, 1989), p. 73. Backscheider (1999), p. 114.

P. 87

Sartre: Jean-Paul Sartre, *The Family Idiot: Gustave Flaubert* [*L'Idiot de la Famille*, 1971], tr. Carol Cosman (University of Chicago,

1981–7), Preface, pp. x, I, 29, 46. Ellis (2000), pp. 145, 149. France and St Clair, p. 282. Barnes (1984, 1985), p. 86.

P. 88

Erik Erikson: *Young Man Luther* (Knopf, 1958); David Ellis (2000), p. 84. Ellmann, (1973), p. 4.

'Put on the couch': see 'The Historical Growth of Psychobiography' in Dan P. McAdams and R. L. Ochberg, *Psychobiography and Life Narratives* (Duke University Press, 1988), pp. 296–9.

Opposition: Bernard De Voto, 'The Sceptical Biographer', *Harper's Magazine*, January 1933, in Clifford (1962), p. 146.

'Overcome a wound' : Edel (1959, 1973), pp. 91–122.

'Manipulate': Ellmann (1973), pp. 9, 13.

'Different aims': see Nadel (1984), pp. 188 ff; Ellis (2000), Ch. 4; David A. Jopling, 'At the Limits of Biographical Knowledge: Sartre and Levinas', in Donaldson (1992), pp. 78–81.

PP. 88–9

Edel: Leon Edel, *The Life of Henry James* (Penguin Books, 1977), vol. I, pp. 49, 53. This was a two-volume revised and shortened version of his five-volume *Life*, published between 1953 and 1971, later re-revised as *Henry James: A Life* (Harper & Row, 1985).

P. 89

Proust: Ellis (2000), p. 60. George Painter, *Marcel Proust: A Biography* (Chatto & Windus, 2 vols, 1959, 1966–7), vol. I, pp. xiii, 115. See John Halperin, 'The Biographer's Revenge', in Salwak (1996), p. 160.

P. 90

Joyce: Richard Ellmann, *James Joyce* (1959; Oxford University Press, 1966), pp. 525, 692, 559, 452, 390, 756.

P. 91

'Notorious exceptions': see Lawrance Thompson's *Robert Frost* (1964, 1977; Holt Rinehart and Winston, 1981); Henri Troyat's *Tolstoi: A Biography* (Doubleday, 1967); and James Atlas's *Bellow: A Biography* (Random House, 2000).

Chapter 6: Against Biography

P. 93

Baudelaire: see Jefferson (2007), p. 162.

'Bundle of accidents': W. B. Yeats, *Essays and Introductions* (Macmillan, 1961), p. 509.

'perfect artist': T. S. Eliot, 'Tradition and the Individual Talent', 1919, *Selected Essays* (Faber & Faber, 1951), p. 18.

'Biografiend', 'Beogrefright': James Joyce, *Finnegans Wake* (1939), 1.3, 3.12. James Joyce, *A Portrait of the Artist as a Young Man* (Penguin, 1960), pp. 214–15.

PP. 93–4

Modernism and biography: Max Saunders, 'Ford, Eliot, Joyce and the Problems of Literary Biography', in Gould and Staley (1998), p. 151. Jefferson (2007), pp. 258, 359, on the *nouveau roman* and biography. Roland Barthes, 'Death of the Author', *Image, Music, Text*, tr. Stephen Heath (Hill & Wang, 1977), pp. 142–8; Michel Foucault, 'What is an Author?', *Language, Counter-Memory, Practice: Selected Essays and Interviews*, ed. D. F. Bouchard (Cornell University Press, 1977), pp. 113–38. Parke, pp. 30, 142. For discussions of literary theory v. biography, see Parke (1996), p. 30; Edel (1959, 1973), Ch. 3; Nigel Hamilton (2007), Ch. 8.

P. 94

Untheorized: see Ian MacKillop, 'Vignettes: Leavis, Biography and the Body', in Gould and Staley (1998), p. 297; Rhiel and Suchoff (1996), p. 1.

P. 95

'Peeping through the keyhole': Malcolm (1993), p. 8.

P. 96

'Bloodsport': Michiko Kakutani, 'Biography as a Blood Sport', *New York Times*, May 1994, cited in Eakin (1999), p. 170; Louis Menand, 'Lives of Others: The Biography Business', *New Yorker*, 8 August 2007.

'Titillation and shock': Justin Kaplan, 'A Culture of Biography'; Martin Stannard, 'The Necrophiliac Art?'; and Natasha Spender, 'Private and Public Lives', in Salwak (1996), pp. 1–6, 36, 101–6.

'Back fire': Ian Hamilton (1988). Ronald Suresh Roberts, *No Cold Kitchen: A Biography of Nadine Gordimer* (STE Publishers, Johannesburg, 2005); Rachel Donadio, 'Nadine Gordimer and the Hazards of Biography', *New York Times Book Review*, 31 December 2006; Rory Carroll, 'Nobel writer Gordimer... accused of censorship', *Guardian*, 7 August 2004.

P. 98

'Self-defence': Doris Lessing, *Under My Skin* (HarperCollins, 1994; Flamingo, 1995), pp. 11, 14.

'Monsters': Philip Larkin, 'Posterity', 1967, in *High Windows* (Faber, 1974); Carol Ann Duffy, 'The Biographer', *Mean Time*, 1993, in *Selected Poems* (Penguin, 1994), p. 123.

P. 99

Fictional biographers: see Holroyd (2002), p. 16; Jon Stallworthy in Batchelor (1995), pp. 29 ff.; Martin Stannard in Gould and Staley (1998), p. 7.

Zuckerman: Philip Roth, *Exit Ghost* (Cape, 2007), pp. 273, 182, 275.

'net': Barnes (1984, 1985), p. 38.

P. 100

'Owns the facts': Ted Hughes, letter to the *Independent*, 20 April 1989.

Chapter 7: Public Roles

P. 101

'social self': Ellmann (1973), p. 2.

'great man': Maurois (1929), pp. 47–8.

'defensive practices': Erving Goffman, *The Presentation of the Self in Everyday Life* (1959; Pelican Books, 1971), pp. 25, 63.

P. 102

Sartre: Goffman, *op. cit.*, p. 42, citing *Being and Nothingness* (1957).

Browning: Henry James to Alice James, 8 April 1877, and 'The Private Life' (1892), both cited in Philip Horne, *Henry James: A Life in Letters* (Allen Lane, 1999), p. 86.

PP. 102–03

Philosophy and biography: 'two schools', James Conant, 'Philosophy and Biography', in James C. Klagge (ed.), *Wittgenstein: Biography and Philosophy* (Cambridge University Press, 2001), p. 17. 'His work is his life', *op. cit.*, p. 19.

P. 103

Wittgenstein's life: James C. Klagge, 'Introduction', *op. cit.*, pp. ix, xiii. David Wiggins, 'Wittgenstein on Ethics and the Riddle of Life', *Philosophy* 79 (2004): 375. Conant, *op. cit.*, pp. 26, 27, summing up Ray Monk, *Ludwig Wittgenstein: The Duty of Genius* (New York, Free Press, 1990; Penguin, 1991).

PP. 103–04

Ray Monk: 'Philosophical Biography: The Very Idea', in Klagge, *op. cit.*, p. 5; 'Life without Theory: Biography as an Exemplar of Philosophical Understanding', *Poetics Today*, Vol. 28 No. 3 (Fall 2007), p. 528.

P. 104

'enacted narratives': Stephen Mulhall, 'The Enigma of Individuality: Identity, Narrative and Truth in Biography, Autobiography and Fiction', unpublished paper, 2003, citing Alasdair MacIntyre, *After Virtue* (Duckworth, 1981), A. S. Byatt, *The Biographer's Tale* (Chatto & Windus, 2001), and Peter Conradi on writing the biography of Iris Murdoch.

'pure act': Henry James, quoted in Jean Strouse, *Morgan: American Financier* (Random House, 1999), p. xiii.

P. 105

'A shilling life': W. H. Auden, 'Who's Who', 1934, *Collected Shorter Poems, 1927–1957* (Faber & Faber, 1966), p. 78.

P. 106

Morgan: Jean Strouse, *op. cit.*, pp. ix, xiii.

P. 107

Elleke Boehmer, *Nelson Mandela: A Very Short Introduction* (Oxford University Press, 2008), pp. 3–7.

For modern saints' lives, see reference to 'later hagiographies' in Ch. II. On the 40th anniversary of Che Guevara's death, see Jay Ambrose, *The Washington Examiner*, cited in *The Week*, 20 October 2007, p. 14.

PP. 107–111

Nelson: N. A. M. Roger, 'Nelson, Horatio, Viscount Nelson', *Oxford DNB*, Vol. 40. John Sugden, *Nelson: A Dream of Glory* (Cape, 2004), pp. 1–13, 787.

P. 111

'history's butlers': Holroyd (2002), p. 5.

Lord Haw-Haw: Rebecca West, *The Meaning of Treason* (Viking, 1947).

Mosley: Nicholas Mosley, *Oswald Mosley: Rules of the Game* and *Beyond the Pale* (Secker & Warburg, 2 vols, 1982, 1983), pp. I, 178.

PP. 111–12

Stalin: Alan Bullock, *Hitler and Stalin, Parallel Lives* (HarperCollins, 1991), p. 801. Simon Sebag Montefiore, *Stalin: The Court of the Red*

Tzar (Weidenfeld & Nicolson, 2004), *Young Stalin* (Weidenfeld & Nicolson, 2008).

P. 113

Shostakovich: 'sweeping platitudes': Laurel E. Fay, *Shostakovich: A Life* (Oxford University Press, 2000), p. 104. 'Soviet humanism': 'Shostakovich', Grove's *Dictionary of Music and Musicians* (Oxford University Press, 2001), pp. 290–300. 'Volkov's reliability': *A Shostakovich Casebook*, ed. M. H. Brown (Indiana University Press, 2005), pp. 19, 81, 315, 370. 'Speculation': Elizabeth Wilson, *Shostakovich: A Life Remembered* (Faber, 1994), p. xi. 'The man from the myths': Fay, p. 2.

P. 115

'Dresden bombings': Christopher Norris, 'Shostakovich: Politics and Musical Language', in *Shostakovich: The Man and His Music*, ed. Christopher Norris (Lawrence and Wishart, 1982), p. 179. 'Emotional breakdown': Fay, p. 216. 'Autobiographical' quartet: Solomon Volkov, *Testimony: The Memoirs of Dmitri Shostakovich*, tr. A. W. Buis (Hamish Hamilton, 1979), p. 118. Galina and Maxim: interviewed in Michael Ardov (ed.), *Memories of Shostakovich*, tr. R. Kelly and M. Meylac (Short Books, 2004), p. 158. 'Dark forces': Fay, p. 219.

P. 116

'Subterfuge': Grove's, p. 290, Elizabeth Wilson, p. 126. 'Pianissimo': Fay, p. 103. 'Our business': Volkov, p. 140.

P. 117

Marilyn: 'legacy': Mike Evans, *Marilyn Handbook* (MQ Publications, 2004), jacket-copy. 'Homicide': Donald H. Wolfe, *The Assassination of Marilyn Monroe* (Sphere, 1998), p. 575.

PP. 117–21

'Star biographies': Richard Dyer, *Heavenly Bodies: Film Stars and Society* (Macmillan, 1986), p. 11. 'Drawn to her': Michelle Morgan, *Marilyn Monroe: Private and Undisclosed* (Constable, 2007), p. 9. 'Either/or': Sarah Churchwell, *The Many Lives of Marilyn Monroe* (Granta, 2004), pp. 8, 194. 'Cornucopia': Norman Mailer, *Marilyn* (Hodder & Stoughton, 1973). 'Mannequin': Joyce Carol Oates, *Blonde* (HarperCollins, 2000). 'Her prison': Gloria Steinem, *Marilyn* (Gollancz, 1987), p. 154. 'Emblematic': Julian Barnes, 'Requiem for a Goddess', *Observer*, 22 February 1987. 'Ugly side': Anthony Summers, *Goddess: The Secret Lives of Marilyn Monroe*

(Gollancz, 1985), pp. 83, 221, 394. 'Freaks': see Backscheider (1999), Ch. 5. 'Strips of film': Keith Hartley, *Warhol: A Celebration of Life ... And Death*, National Galleries of Scotland, 2007, Catalogue 31.

Chapter 8: Telling the Story

P. 122

Hermione Lee, *Virginia Woolf* (Chatto & Windus, 1996; Vintage, 1997), p. 3.

P. 123

Argument against: see Mark Kinkead-Weekes, 'Writing Lives Forward', in France and St Clair (2002), pp. 238, 253. R. F. Foster, *W. B. Yeats: A Life, I: The Apprentice Mage 1865–1914* (Oxford University Press, 1997), p. xxvi. James Olney, 'The Taking of a Life: Some Versions of Biography', *The Cincinnati Review*, Spring 2005: 73–4.

PP. 124–5

Beginnings: Richard Holmes, *Shelley: The Pursuit* (Weidenfeld and Nicolson, 1974; Quartet, 1976). Victoria Glendinning, *Rebecca West: A Life* (Weidenfeld and Nicolson, 1987), p. 1. Maynard Mack, *Alexander Pope: A Life* (Yale University Press, 1985), p. 3. Nicholas Shakespeare, *Bruce Chatwin* (Vintage, 2000), p. 1. Arnold Rampersad, *Ralph Ellison: A Biography* (Knopf, 2007), p. 3.

P. 126

'Lives of the obscure': Virginia Woolf, 'Lives of the Obscure', *The Essays of Virginia Woolf*, ed. Andrew McNeillie (Hogarth Press, 1986–), vol. 4.

'Uncover a past': Jenny Uglow, 'Friends Reunited', *Guardian*, 30 April 2005, pp. 34–5.

'Who will speak?': Carole Ferrier, 'Resisting Authority', in Donaldson (1992), p. 104.

PP. 126–7

'Hidden histories': Jean Strouse, *Alice James: A Biography* (Houghton Mifflin, 1980); Claire Tomalin, *The Invisible Woman* (Viking, 1990); Brenda Maddox, *Nora: The Real Life of Molly Bloom* (Houghton Mifflin, 1988); Alison Light, *Mrs Woolf and the Servants* (Penguin Fig Tree, 2007). Virginia Woolf, *A Room of One's Own* (1929; Penguin, 1993), p. 88.

P. 127

'Constraints': Heilbrun (1989), pp. 28, 30.

'Feminist project': Kay Ferres, 'Gender, Biography and the Public
   Sphere', in France and St Clair (2002), p. 307, citing Maria Pia
   Lara, *Feminist Narratives in the Public Sphere* (Cambridge
   University Press, 1998).

'Past tenses': Steedman (1992), pp. 160–4.

'Women's stories': Backscheider (1999), pp. 132, 11, 147.

P. 128

'Access to privacy': Alison Booth, 'Biographical Criticism and the "Great
   Woman of Letters"' in *Contesting the Subject*, ed. William Epstein
   (Purdue University Press, 1986), p. 89. See also Alison Booth, *How
   to Make It as a Woman* (University of Chicago, 2004).

P. 129

Sexton: Diane Wood Middlebrook, *Anne Sexton* (Houghton Mifflin,
   1990).

'Public life': Kay Ferres, p. 303, and James Walter, 'The Solace of
   Doubt? Biographical Methodology after the Short Twentieth
   Century', in France and St Clair (2002), pp. 330–1, both citing
   Steedman (1992), pp. 164–6.

Lives of Jane Austen: see Kathryn Sutherland, *Jane Austen's Textual
   Lives* (Oxford University Press, 2005); Claire Harman, *Jane's
   Fame: How Jane Austen Conquered the World*, Canongate, 2009.

P. 130

Shakespeare titles: Peter Ackroyd (Chatto & Windus, 2005); Stephen
   Greenblatt (Cape, 2004); James Shapiro (Faber, 2005).

Lives of Keats: Andrew Motion, *Keats* (Faber, 1997); Robert Gittings,
   John Keats (Heinemann, 1968).

Contents pages:

Jean Yves Tadié, *Marcel Proust*, tr. Euan Cameron (1996; Viking,
   2000), p. ix. Adrian Frazier, *George Moore* (Yale University Press,
   2000), p. v.

P. 132

'Watershed': John Halperin, *The Life of Jane Austen* (Harvester, 1984),
   p. 124. 'Celibate': Leon Edel, *Henry James: A Life* (Harper & Row,
   1985), p. 16. 'Techniques of fiction': Edel (1959, 1973), p. 151.

On illness and biography: Ellis (2000), Ch. 5.

Turgenev: V. S. Pritchett, *The Gentle Barbarian: The Life and Work of
   Turgenev* (Chatto & Windus, 1977), p. 9.

P. 133

Empson: John Haffenden, *William Empson: Among the Mandarins* (Oxford University Press, 2005), vol. I, p. 9.

Larkin: Andrew Motion, *Philip Larkin: A Writer's Life* (Faber, 1993), p. 266.

Gill: Fiona MacCarthy, *Eric Gill* (Faber, 1989), p. viii.

Hemingway: Michael Reynolds, *Hemingway: The Final Years* (Norton, 1999), p. 360.

P. 134

Bellow: James Atlas, *Saul Bellow* (Random House, 2000), pp. 284, 372.

'Autobiography': Maurois (1929), p. 112.

Thoreau: Richard Lebeaux, 'Thoreau's Lives, Lebeaux's Lives' (Baron and Pletsch, 1985), p. 247.

P. 135

Lehmann: Selina Hastings, *Rosamond Lehmann: A Life* (Chatto & Windus, 2002); see Lee (2005, 2008), pp. 145–8.

Beckett: Deirdre Bair, *Samuel Beckett: A Biography* (Cape, 1978), p. 10.

Colette: Judith Thurman, *Secrets of the Flesh: A Life of Colette* (Knopf, 1999), p. xiii.

On Sherry and Greene, see James Olney, 'The Taking of a Life: Some Versions of Biography', *The Cincinnati Review*, Spring 2005, pp. 73–4.

On wrestling, see Holroyd's tragi-comic account of his battle over Shaw with the scholar Dan Lawrence (2002), pp. 169–83.

'To Bring the Dead to Life': Robert Graves, 1936, in *Collected Poems* (Cassell, 1938).

PP. 136–7

'Micro-biography': James Shapiro, *1599: A Year in the Life of William Shakespeare* (Faber, 2005), pp. xvii, xix.

P. 137

'The little they know': see Ellis (2000), pp. 120, 185, note 6, on Samuel Schoenbaum's account of the many versions of Shakespeare's life.

PP. 137–8

VIII, p. 93 Death of Hamnet: 'Mad Danish prince': Anthony Burgess, *Shakespeare* (Cape, 1970; Penguin, 1971), p. 65. 21st-century versions: Charles Nicholl, *The Lodger: Shakespeare on Silver Street* (Allen Lane, 2007; Penguin, 2008), pp. 6, 15; Jonathan Bate, *Soul of the Age: The Life, Mind and World of William Shakespeare* (Viking, 2008). 'We just don't know': Shapiro, *op. cit.*, pp. 14–15, 260–1, 309–58. 'Dispassionate': Park Honan, *Shakespeare: A Life* (Oxford University Press, 1998), pp. 235, 236. 'Deep wound': Stephen Greenblatt, *Will in the World: How Shakespeare became Shakespeare* (Cape, 2004), pp. 290, 311, 318. 'He may, or may not': Peter Ackroyd, *Shakespeare: The Biography* (Chatto & Windus, 2005), pp. 270–1. See Lois Potter, 'Having Our Will: Imagination in Recent Shakespearian Biographies', *Shakespeare Survey* 58 (Cambridge University Press, 2005), pp. 1–8, for a comparative account of Honan, Greenblatt, and others.

PP. 138–40
Narrating the deaths: see Lee, 'How to End it All', (2005, 2008), pp. 200–18.

Bibliography

Main titles referred to are given here in full, and in abbreviated form in the Chapter References.

Aaron, Daniel (ed.), *Studies in Biography* (Harvard University Press, 1978)

Altick, Richard, *Lives and Letters: A History of Literary Biography in England and America* (Knopf, 1965)

Anderson, Judith, *Biographical Truth: The Representation of Historical Persons in Tudor-Stuart Writing* (Yale University Press, 1984)

Backscheider, Paula, *Reflections on Biography* (Oxford University Press, 1999)

Barnes, Julian, *Flaubert's Parrot* (Cape, 1984; Picador 1985)

Baron, Samuel H., and Pletsch, Carl (eds.), *Introspection in Biography* (The Analytic Press, University of North Carolina, 1985)

Batchelor, John (ed.), *The Art of Literary Biography* (The Clarendon Press, 1995)

Bell, Susan G., and Yalom, M. (eds.), *Revealing Lives: Autobiography, Biography and Gender* (New York State University Press, 1990)

Bertaux, Daniel (ed.), *Biography and Society: The Life History Approach in the Social Sciences* (Sage, 1981)

Boswell, James, 'Advertisements' and 'Preface' to *The Life of Samuel Johnson* (London, 1791; a new edition corrected by J. W. Fleeman, ed. R. W. Chapman, Oxford University Press, 1953; *The Life of Johnson*, 1791, Oxford University Press, World's Classics)

Bromwich, David, 'The Uses of Biography', *Yale Review*, 73 (Winter 1984): 161–75

Broughton, Trev Lynn, *Men of Letters, Writing Lives* (Routledge, 1999)

Carlyle, Thomas, Review of Croker's edition of Boswell's *The Life of Samuel Johnson*; Review of Lockhart's *The Life of Scott*, see Clifford, James

Clifford, James, *Biography as an Art: Selected Criticism, 1590–1960* (Oxford University Press, 1962)

Cockshut, A. O. J., *Truth to Life: The Art of Biography in the Nineteenth Century* (Collins, 1974)

Daghlian, Philip (ed.), *Essays in 18th Century Biography* (Indiana University Press, 1988)

Donaldson, Ian, Read, Peter, and Walter, James (eds.), *Shaping Lives: Reflections on Biography* (Humanities Research Centre, Canberra, 1992)

Eakin, Paul J., *How Our Lives Become Stories* (Cornell University Press, 1999); *The Ethics of Life Writing* (Cornell University Press, 2004)

Edel, Leon, *Literary Biography* (Indiana University Press, 1959, 1973); *Writing Lives: Principia Biographia* (Norton, 1984)

Ellis, David, *Literary Lives: Biography and the Search for Understanding* (Oxford University Press, 2000)

Ellmann, Richard, *Golden Codgers: Biographical Speculations* (Oxford University Press, 1973)

Empson, William, *Using Biography* (Chatto & Windus, 1984)

Epstein, William H., *Recognizing Biography* (Pennsylvania University Press, 1987)

France, Peter, and St Clair, William (eds.), *Mapping Lives: The Uses of Biography* (British Academy and Oxford University Press, 2002)

Gaskell, Elizabeth, *The Life of Charlotte Brontë* (1857; ed. Jenny Uglow, Everyman, 1992)

Gosse, Edmund, 'Biography', *Encylopaedia Britannica*, 11th edition (1910–11), pp. 952–3; *Father and Son* (Heinemann, 1907); *Tallemant des Réaux, or the Art of Miniature Biography* (Oxford University Press, 1925)

Gould, Warwick, and Staley, Thomas (eds.), *Writing the Lives of Writers* (Macmillan, 1998)

Hamilton, Ian, *In Search of J. D. Salinger* (Heinemann, 1988); *Keepers of the Flame: Literary Estates and the Rise of Biography* (Hutchinson, 1992; Pimlico, 1993)

Hamilton, Nigel, *Biography: A Brief History* (Harvard University Press, 2007)

Heilbrun, Carolyn, *Writing a Woman's Life* (Norton, 1988; Ballantyne Books, 1989)

Hoberman, Ruth, *Modernizing Lives: Experiments in English Biography 1918–1939* (Southern Illinois University Press, 1987)

Holmes, Richard, *Footsteps: Adventures of a Romantic Biographer* (Hodder & Stoughton, 1985; Flamingo, 1995); *Dr Johnson & Mr Savage* (Hodder & Stoughton, 1993)

Holroyd, Michael, *Works on Paper* (Little, Brown, 2002)

Homberger, Eric, and Charmley, John (eds.), *The Troubled Face of Biography* (St Martin's Press, 1988)

Honan, Park, *Authors' Lives* (St Martin's Press, 1990)

James, Henry, *The Aspern Papers*, 1888 (Everyman, 1994)

Jefferson, Ann, *Biography and the Question of Literature in France* (Oxford University Press, 2007)

Johnson, Samuel, 'On Biography', *The Rambler*, 13 October 1750, No. 60; *The Idler*, 24 November 1759, No. 84, in Clifford, James. Roger Lonsdale (ed.), *Johnson's Lives of the Poets* (Oxford University Press, 2006)

Jolly, Margaretta (ed.), *Encylopaedia of Life Writing* (Fitzroy Dearborn, 2 vols, 2001)

Kendall, Paul Murray, *The Art of Biography* (Allen & Unwin, 1965; Norton, 1985)

Lee, Hermione, *Body Parts: Essays on Life-Writing* (Chatto & Windus, 2005; Pimlico, 2008)

Lee, Sidney, *Principles of Biography* (Cambridge University Press, 1911); *The Perspective of Biography* (Cambridge University Press, 1918)

Malcolm, Janet, *The Silent Woman: Sylvia Plath and Ted Hughes* (Picador, 1993)

Marcus, Laura, *Auto/Biographical Discourses: Theory, Criticism, Practice* (Manchester University Press, 1994)

Maurois, André, *Aspects of Biography* (1928; tr. S. C. Roberts, Cambridge University Press, 1929)

Meyers, Jeffrey (ed.), *The Craft of Literary Biography* (Macmillan, 1985)

Miller, Lucasta, *The Brontë Myth* (Cape, 2001, 2005)

Nadel, Ira Bruce, *Biography: Fiction, Fact and Form* (Macmillan, 1984)

Nicolson, Harold, *The Development of English Biography* (Hogarth Press, 1928)

Novarr, David, *The Lines of Life: Theories of Biography, 1880–1970* (Purdue University Press, 1986)

O'Connor, Ulick, *Biographers and the Art of Biography* (Quartet Books, 1991)

Oliphant, Margaret, 'The Ethics of Biography', *Contemporary Review*, XLIV (July 1883)

Origo, Iris, *A Need to Testify* (Harcourt Brace, 1984)

Parke, Catherine N., *Biography: Writing Lives* (Twayne, 1996; Routledge, 2002)

Redford, Bruce, *Designing the Life of Johnson* (Oxford University Press, 2002)

Rhiel, Mary, and Suchoff, David (eds.), *The Seductions of Biography* (Routledge, 1996)

Salwak, Dale (ed.), *The Literary Biography: Problems and Solutions* (Iowa University Press, 1996)

Shelston, Alan, *Biography* (Methuen, 1977)

Sisman, Adam, *Boswell's Presumptuous Task* (Hamish Hamilton, 2000)

Stauffer, Donald, *English Biography before 1700* (Harvard University Press, 1930); *The Art of Biography in 18th-Century England* (Princeton University Press, 1941)

Steedman, Carolyn, *Past Tenses: Essays on Writing Autobiography and History* (Rivers Oram Press, 1992)

Stephen, Leslie, 'National Biography', in *Studies of a Biographer*, vol. 1 (Duckworth, 1898)

Strachey, Lytton, *Eminent Victorians* (Chatto & Windus, 1918; Oxford University Press World's Classics, 2003)

Symons, Arthur, *The Quest for Corvo: An Experiment in Biography* (Cassell, 1934, 1955)

Tomalin, Claire, *The Invisible Woman: The Story of Nelly Ternan and Charles Dickens* (Penguin, 1991)

Wagner-Martin, Linda, *Telling Women's Lives: The New Biography* (Rutgers University Press, 1994)

Wendorf, Richard, *The Elements of Life: Biography and Portrait Painting in Stuart and Georgian England* (Oxford University Press, 1990)

Whittemore, Reed, *Pure Lives: The Early Biographers* (Johns Hopkins University Press, 1983); *Whole Lives: Shapers of Modern Biography* (Johns Hopkins University Press, 1989)

Woolf, Virginia, 'The New Biography' (1927), 'The Art of Biography' (1939); *Collected Essays*, ed. L. Woolf (London, Chatto & Windus, 1966–7)

Publisher's Acknowledgements

'Biography' taken from *The Collected Poems of Ian Hamilton* © The Estate of Ian Hamilton and reproduced by permission of Faber and Faber Ltd. *Keepers of the Flame: Literary Estates and the Rise of Biography*, permission granted by Aitken Alexander. © Ian Hamilton Estate. 'The Silent Woman' by Janet Malcolm, permission granted by Pan Macmillan, London. Copyright © Janet Malcolm, 1994. 'Posterity' by Philip Larkin, from *High Windows*, 1974, permission granted by Faber and Faber Ltd/ © The Estate (UK rights) and Farrar, Straus, and Giroux, LLC (US rights). 'The Biographer' by Carol Ann Duffy, from *Mean Time*, 1993, published by Anvil Press Poetry, 1993, new edition 1998. 'Flaubert's Parrot' by Julian Barnes, copyright © Julian Barnes, 1984, permission granted by United Agents on behalf of Julian Barnes. 'A Shilling Life Will Give You All The Facts', by W.H. Auden, from *Selected Poems, Expanded Edition* by W.H. Auden, edited by Edward Mendelson, copyright © Edward Mendelson, William Meredith and Monroe K. Spears, Executors of the Estate of W. H. Auden, 1979, 2007. Used by permission of Faber and Faber Ltd (UK rights) and Vintage Books, a division of Random House, Inc (US rights). 'To Bring the Dead to Life' by Robert Graves, copyright © Robert Graves, from *Complete Poems in One Volume*, Carcanet Press Limited.

The publisher and the author apologize for any errors or omissions in the above list. If contacted they will be happy to rectify these at the earliest opportunity.

Index

D

E

F